Clinical Counselling in Schools

Too often in education there is a split between those concerned with children's personal and emotional well-being and those focusing on academic achievement. At a time when counselling in schools is on the increase, working towards an integration of the personal and the academic is paramount.

Clinical Counselling in Schools provides counsellors, educational psychologists, teachers, teacher-trainers and other interested professionals with essential insights into how counselling best works within a school. Covering a wide range of problems encountered in schools, the contributors – all experienced school counsellors – show how the context, be it state or public, primary or secondary, mainstream or special school, needs to be acknowledged in order to support and foster the emotional and academic welfare of the child.

Using a wealth of clinical information, *Clinical Counselling in Schools* is timely and essential reading for counsellors and all educational professionals who wish to utilise the full potential of counselling in the context of schools.

Nick Barwick has worked in the educational sector for fifteen years, first as a teacher in secondary and tertiary institutions, then as a student counsellor. He now works as a counsellor at the Guildhall School of Music and Drama. He is Associate Editor of *Psychodynamic Counselling*.

Clinical Counselling in Schools

Edited by Nick Barwick

BRUNNER-ROUTLEDGE
ALERE FLAMMA'M
Taylor & Francis Group

First published 2000
by Routledge
11 New Fetter Lane, London EC4P 4EE

Simultaneously published in the USA and Canada
by Taylor & Francis Inc
325 Chestnut Street, Philadelphia PA 19106

Reprinted 2001
by Brunner-Routledge
27 Church Road, Hove, East Sussex BN3 2A

Brunner-Routledge is an imprint of the Taylor & Francis Group

Typeset in Times by Keystroke, Jacaranda Lodge, Wolverhampton
Printed and bound in Great Britain by St Edmundsbury Press, Bury St
Edmunds, Suffolk

British Library Cataloguing in Publication Data
A catalogue record for this book is available from the British Library

Library of Congress Cataloging in Publication Data
Clinical counselling in schools / edited by Nick Barwick.
      p.   cm. — (Clinical counselling in context)
   Includes bibliographical references and index.
   1. School children—Mental health services. 2. School psychology.
   3. Clinical psychology. I. Title: Clinical counselling in schools.
   II. Barwick, Nick, 1959– III. Series.
LB3430 .C57 2000
371.4′6–dc21   99–058558

ISBN 0–415–20516–6 (hbk)
ISBN 0–415–20517–4 (pbk)

Contents

Contributors

Sarah Adams has taught in mainstream and special schools, working in the latter also as a drama and movement therapist. A UKCP registered educational therapist, she now works for the Child and Adolescent Mental Health Service in Brighton.

Nick Barwick taught English in the state sector for fifteen years. Having counselled part time in several post-sixteen colleges, he now works as a student counsellor at the Guildhall School of Music and Drama. He is Associate Editor of *Psychodynamic Counselling*, and presently training as a group analyst.

Hamish Canham is a child and adolescent psychotherapist working at the Tavistock Clinic, London. His time is divided between clinical work and teaching. He is Co-Course Tutor of the Tavistock's MA in 'Emotional factors in learning and teaching'.

Florence Heller worked in the UK and abroad as a social case worker. Taking a Master's degree in counselling and psychotherapy at Regent's College, she counselled in a London secondary school for nine years. She now works for Hibiscus, an agency helping foreign national women prisoners.

Elizabeth Herrick, following early careers in nursing and accountancy, taught in secondary schools with disaffected pupils. Training as an educational psychologist, she worked in Hampshire for five years before becoming Senior Educational Psychologist in Southampton.

Philip Hewitt has worked in education for many years - in social work training, at City University Counselling Service and currently as Head of Counselling at Westminster School. A member of the British Association of Psychotherapists and the Forum for Independent

Psychotherapists, he is a UKCP and BCP registered psychoanalytic psychotherapist and works in private practice.

Hilary Hickmore has worked as an educational psychologist for Hampshire LEA for eleven years, specialising in emotional and behavioural difficulties. Training in integrative arts psychotherapy, she gains replenishment and balance at her rural home with her two children, her husband and a large collection of birds, animals and fish.

Gill Morton is a teacher and UKCP registered educational therapist working with children and families in the Education Unit of The Marlborough Family Service and privately in schools. She contributes to the Forum for the Advancement of Educational Therapy and Therapeutic Teaching's Training in Educational Therapy.

Miranda Ommanney trained as an actor at the Royal Academy of Dramatic Art and for many years followed a career in theatre and television. She was Senior Counsellor at Queen Mary's College, Basingstoke and is now Student Counsellor at Lord Mayor Treloar School and College.

June Platts is a UKCP registered psychotherapist, accredited by the British Association for Cognitive-Behavioural Psychotherapy. Working as a psychotherapist and counsellor with the NHS, Social Services and in private practice, she specialises in treating young people with emotional and behavioural problems.

Peter Sharp taught for seven years before being seconded to the Institute of Education and to the Tavistock Clinic where he trained as an educational psychologist. Currently Principal Educational Psychologist in Southampton, he lives in the New Forest with his wife Lindsey and their two daughters, Chloe and Poppy.

Jan Symes worked as a nurse and social worker prior to training as a counsellor. Having counselled for Brook Advisory Service and University College Hospital, for five years she was Head of Counselling for the Employee Assistance Programme, British Airways, and is currently Head of Counselling at Lord Mayor Treloar School and College.

Ferelyth Watt qualified as a teacher in 1980 and worked in primary schools, with adolescents on a school leaver's project and as a peripatetic special needs teacher. As a child and adolescent psycho-therapist, she now works in a child, family and adolescent mental health team in the Tower Hamlets Healthcare NHS Trust and as a schools counsellor.

Yuki Williamson is a psychodynamic counsellor and trainer. She has worked with young people both privately and for child and family psychiatric services and is interested in women's issues, marital therapy and groupwork. She is currently writing her Master's dissertation and co-authoring a book on mid-life.

Biddy Youell is a child and adolescent psychotherapist working at the Tavistock Clinic, London. Her time is divided between clinical work and teaching. She is Co-Course Tutor of the Tavistock's MA course in 'Emotional factors in learning and teaching'.

Acknowledgements

I am hugely indebted to both Carol Maynard and Yuki Williamson for their advice, help and generous support in the process of editing.

I should also like to acknowledge the following who have kindly helped in the preparation of this book:

Polly Burridge, Sandy Burnfield, Anne Casimir, Jenny Dover-Councell, Pat French, Ann Heyno, Helen High, Jenny Leggatt, Liza Lomax, Ellen Noonan, Gillian Salmon, Ferelyth Watt.

A note on the use of pronouns

There is always a problem about the use of the generic pronoun. Contributors to this book, both male and female, have found various ways of dealing with this. In a book which celebrates diversity, I have not interfered in this respect.

Permissions

I would like to thank the following publishers:

Carfax for permission to quote from Colleen McLaughlin (1999) 'Counselling in schools: looking back and looking forward' *British Journal of Guidance and Counselling* 27(1): 13–22.

Routledge for permission to reproduce substantially revised versions of two articles (Chapters 5 and 11) previously published in *Psychodynamic Counselling*.

Ferelyth Watt (1994) 'Is it safe enough to learn?' *Psychodynamic Counselling* 1(1): 119–136.

Nick Barwick (1995) 'Pandora's box: an investigation of essay anxiety in adolescents' *Psychodynamic Counselling* 1(4): 560–575.

The websites for the above journals can be found at www.tandf.co.uk

Introduction

Nick Barwick

Growing up is difficult. Distressing life events make it more so. Bullying, bereavement, family divisions, substance abuse, physical, sexual and emotional abuse, sexual and racial harassment, unwanted pregnancy, isolation, suicidal feelings – all these issues and more invade the lives of many young people, disrupting school life and the ability to learn. An important role of counselling in schools is to support such children through these crises, helping them to deal more effectively with the pain they bear. Emotional relief may also then better allow them to focus upon the educational tasks at hand. Thus, implicit in the task of counselling in a school context is a dual aim: the psychological *and* educational well-being of the child.

In fact three types or 'levels' of counselling are often identified as occurring in schools: the immediate, the intermediate and the intensive (Hamblin 1993). The first describes an environment in which teachers, using 'counselling skills', sustain a non-judgemental and empathic relationship with their pupils in order to both help identify those experiencing difficulties and promote a 'positive climate for learning' for all. The second level refers to the activities of those teachers who, as well as having responsibility for pupil development as part of the care curriculum, utilise basic counsellor training to work with troubled pupils and, if necessary, refer them for specialist help. This leaves the third, intensive level: the province of the specialist – the clinical counsellor.

This hierarchical description is both useful and misleading. It is useful because it identifies clinical counselling in schools as an area of specialism; one which, dealing as it does with the confusing and painful intricacies of young people's emotional lives, is a complex enterprise, not to be undertaken lightly or without sound training and supervisory scrutiny and support. It is misleading, as it can cast the counsellor as adjunct *to* rather than participant *in* the life of a school; one whose sole function it is to act as receptacle for the most disturbed and disturbing, and often, particularly with disruptive children, as precarious shelter at the last stop before exclusion. Dealing with the individual needs of disturbed and disturbing children is clearly a vital part of the school counsellor's role. Such children tend to bring to school personal problems which, though interfering with both their and sometimes others' academic and social learning, have their source elsewhere. Yet school is no neutral ground and the tasks of teaching and learning, as well as other complex social interactions that make up the life of a school, have an impact upon each and every child and adult within it and are charged with meaning. In short, the problem may not be in the child *alone* but in the interaction between child and context (the school).

The contributors to this book approach their work from many different theoretical perspectives – behavioural, cognitive-behavioural, Gestalt/TA, person-centred, psychodynamic, systemic – using art, stories, structured and unstructured talk and play. Yet whatever their perspective, each keeps the context in which they work firmly in view. The ramifications of this 'context-sightedness' are varied. Some counsellors, though resisting the practical impingement of school context upon the therapeutic work, utilise it as material for the process of therapeutic thinking. Others, seeking to make fuller use of school (and family) resources, broaden the counselling boundaries in order to buttress and extend the therapeutic work. And then there are some who, taking a more proactive approach, forgo the consulting room and, instead, work in deliberate fashion to create therapeutic opportunities within the ordinary life of the school. Whatever the approach, whatever the theoretical disposition, common to the rich tapestry of clinical practice depicted in these chapters is that the context, whether it informs or transforms the counselling process, is never long or far from mind.

In a lively opening chapter, drawing on psychodynamic thought with a touch of Charles Dickens, Hamish Canham and Biddy Youell set the contextual stage, immediately highlighting how complex and emotionally charged the process of learning is. The way we learn is *learnt* – in infancy in relationship to the mother and later through relations with the whole family – long before we arrive at school. And then, just when it seems the child's learning efforts reach solid ground, along comes adolescence!

A focus common to chapters 2 to 4 is the management of boundaries in school counselling. In Florence Heller's lucid description of her work with deprived children in an inner city school, she argues against a 'purist' approach and for the need to be open to appropriate collaboration with teaching staff, in an effort to provide the type of nurturing conditions Winnicott refers to as 'the holding environment'. Working from a person-centred perspective, Miranda Ommanney and Jan Symes echo many of these sentiments. Their vital work with young people with severe disabilities is movingly portrayed, as they reflect upon the particular difficulties experienced by the counsellor in maintaining 'core conditions' and the right balance of intimacy and distance in work that to many might seem unbearable. Last in this set is Philip Hewitt's subtle and often poetic description of his work in a public school. Here, a rigorous though uncomfortable holding of the therapeutic 'membrane' of confidentiality forces the counsellor to think about the painful, isolating feelings experienced by the client. It is a chapter which offers rich examples of how thinking about context can inform the counselling without transforming it.

To some degree, chapters 5 and 6 do, however, describe clinical work transformed by context. This is partly because of the roles these authors play within the contexts in which they work. Ferelyth Watt, working as a psychodynamically trained area support teacher, gives a detailed, probing account of some difficult, relatively long-term, intensive counselling. Working with children in class as well as individually, she shows how context can be used both to gather important information and achieve the desired therapeutic effect.

Watt's theme is the need for safety if learning is to take place. Sarah Adams takes up this theme in her engaging, vivid description of drama therapy with children in an EBD school (a school for children with emotional and behavioural difficulties). In particular, she explores how the therapeutic use of stories can complement her work as a teacher, and help establish a 'secure base' for those children whose 'insecure attachments' frustrate their ability to socialise and learn.

June Platts and Yuki Williamson bring a different perspective – the cognitive-behavioural approach (CBT). In a clear, uncluttered account, they argue forcefully for the cultural fit between educational aims and methods, and CBT work. Both are concerned with clarity of thinking, unfettered by 'irrational beliefs', and both employ collaborative methods in which pupils/clients are encouraged to take responsibility for their learning and growth.

Chapters 8 and 9 are both contributions of educational psychologists. Drawing on Gestalt therapy and transactional analysis, Hilary Hickmore argues convincingly and enthusiastically for the use of art and play as a powerful means of engaging disaffected children and enabling them to communicate deeply troubling issues of which they themselves may not even be aware. Further, promoting an integrative approach, she sees such work as playing an essential part in the design and implementation of children's individual education plans. In contrast, Peter Sharp and Elizabeth Herrick, responding to teacher requests for help with difficult students, employ a group approach, based mainly upon behavioural and cognitive-behavioural principles. Their exciting and innovative work is radically proactive, promoting 'emotional literacy' and deliberately including teachers in an effort to stimulate a systemic shift in the way that 'problem anger' is dealt with in schools.

Complementing yet contrasting with Sharp and Herrick's approach is that described by Gill Morton. Again, working with groups, the fascinating clinical material she presents gives vivid insights into many of the emotional difficulties blocking children's learning. As with the previous authors, she adopts a deliberate policy of working with teachers, since her aim is not only to provide a space for children's thinking but also to contribute to the development of teachers' understanding and therapeutic repertoires.

Singly rather than in groups, in the final chapter I turn to the most common form of writing exercise required of older children – the essay. Using object relations theory, I describe my attempts to understand what hinders able children in fulfilling their academic potential in this field. I suggest that the curiously ordinary exercise of essay-writing can become, for the adolescent, the dramatic stage upon which deep ambivalence about aggression and the prospect of leaving home are acted out to the detriment of academic success.

In a cogent and useful review of the history and present state of school counselling, Colleen McLaughlin (1999: 21) berates a recent 'regression' to 'previous views of counselling as the province of specialists', concluding that:

> The evidence seems to be that we need to develop the role, skills and pedagogy of counselling, not restrict it. The need of young people in the context of a personally and socially complex society, which is aiming to become a learning society, requires us to develop and integrate counselling theory and skills into the role of all teachers, not compartmentalise it.

I concur with this vision, though, as teacher *and* clinical counsellor, I do not berate the return of specialists, as long as they have a role that allows them to be a participant *in* rather than an adjunct *to* the school. More accurately, to misappropriate a term used by Harry Stack Sullivan (1954),

I would suggest that the role required of the clinical counsellor in the context of school is that of 'participant-observer'; one who, being an observer, may offer a safe space characterised by the necessary illusion of being outside the context, yet, being a participant – one who recognises that, inevitably, they are part of a context and are implicated in the life of the school – may utilise this position to good therapeutic effect. In this way, a school counsellor acts as both receptacle and vessel: receptacle, because he or she must be open to what is poured into them; vessel, because what is poured in may, in due course and in a different, more processed form, be poured back. At times, what is poured back is an individual who, having had a safe space to consider new ways of thinking, feeling and behaving, may better negotiate the intricate relationships involved in the process of learning in the context of school. At others, what might be poured back is *not* the individual, but a different perspective regarding the interactional life of the school. Whichever it is, individual or perspective, systemic thinking suggests there is a vital connection between the two, since 'Every part of a system is so related to its fellow parts that a change in one part will cause a change in all' (Watzlawick *et al*. 1967: 123). In this way, clinical counsellors who properly take note of the context in which they work and breathe may contribute something vital not only to the life of the child but also to the life of an effective and affectively oriented school.[1]

Note

1　I borrow the notion of 'affective education' from Lang (1995).

References

Hamblin, D. H. (1993) *The Teacher and Counselling* (2nd edn), Oxford: Simon and Schuster.

Lang, P. (1995) 'International perspectives in pastoral Care', in R. Best, P. Lang, C. Lodge and C. Watkins (eds) *Pastoral Care and Social-Personal Education*, London: Cassell.

McLaughlin, C. (1999) 'Counselling in schools: looking back and looking forward', *British Journal of Guidance & Counselling*, 27(1): 13–22.

Sullivan, H. S. (1954) *The Psychiatric Interview*, New York: W.W. Norton & Co.

Watzlawick, P., Beavin, J. and Jackson, D. (1967) *Pragmatics of Human Communication*, New York: W.W. Norton & Co.

Chapter 1

The developmental and educational context

The emotional experience of learning

Hamish Canham and Biddy Youell

Models of learning

It is no coincidence that the formal schooling of children in this country begins at five, and that there is a transition from primary to secondary school at eleven. These changes in the educational context correspond to transitions in children's development. A child of five is at a point in his life when he is leaving babyhood and early childhood and entering the period known as latency. A child of eleven is poised on the brink of puberty and adolescence. In this chapter, we want to look at the interpenetration of the child's developmental progress and emotional state with the external educational environment.

We also want to draw attention to how models of learning vary at different stages of development. Whatever the age of the child, there is an important distinction to be drawn between the two types of learning distinguished by the psychoanalyst Wilfred Bion, as 'learning about' and 'learning from experience'. The former is characterised by a lack of curiosity and the accumulation of facts and figures; the latter by a gradual making sense of the world through one's own experience of it.

Charles Dickens embodies these contrasting ways of learning in *Hard Times* in the persons of Sissy Jupe, a circus girl, on one hand, and the teacher, Mr M'Choakumchild and the principal, Mr Gradgrind, on the other. As the extract below shows, Mr M'Choakumchild and Mr Gradgrind teach a system of learning based on 'facts' and the accumulation of knowledge in which the role of imagination or 'fancy' is subordinated to the dry, meaningless repetition by rote of the external characteristics of objects. Sissy Jupe breathes life into learning, through a meaningful, personal connection to the subject by using her mind and having independence of thought.

'Now, what I want is, Facts. Teach these boys and girls nothing but Facts. Facts alone are wanted in life. Plant nothing else, and root out everything else. You can only form the minds of reasoning animals upon Facts: nothing else will ever be of any service to them. This is the principle on which I bring up my own children and this is the principle on which I bring up these children. Stick to Facts, Sir!'

This is how Mr Gradgrind expounds his educational system to the schoolmaster Mr M'Choakumchild and his pupils. He sees the children in the classroom as 'little vessels . . . ready to have imperial gallons of facts poured into them until they were full to the brim'.

'Now, let me ask you girls and boys, would you paper a room with representations of horses?'
After a pause, one half of the children cried in chorus, 'Yes, Sir!' Upon which the other half, seeing in the gentleman's face that Yes was wrong, cried out in chorus, 'No, Sir!' – as the custom is in these examinations.
'Of course, No. Why wouldn't you?'
A pause. One corpulent, slow boy with a wheezy manner of breathing, ventured the answer. Because he wouldn't paper a room at all, but would paint it.
'You *must* paper it,' said Thomas Gradgrind, 'whether you like it or not. Don't tell *us* you wouldn't paper it. What do you mean, boy?'
'I'll explain to you then,' said the gentleman, after another and dismal pause, 'why you wouldn't paper a room with representations of horses. Do you ever see horses walking up and down the sides of rooms in reality – in fact? Do you?'
'Yes, Sir!' from one half. 'No, Sir!' from the other.

This stifling of imagination and conviction that there is a right way to view the world is, of course, represented in Mr M'Choakumchild's and Mr Gradgrind's names. Sissy, or Cecilia as Mr Gradgrind calls her, has another view of things.

There being a general conviction by this time that 'No, Sir!' was always the right answer to this gentleman, the chorus of No was very strong. Only a few feeble stragglers said Yes; among them Sissy Jupe.
'Girl number twenty,' said the gentleman, smiling in the calm strength of knowledge.
Sissy blushed, and stood up.

'So you would carpet your room – or your husband's room if you were a grown woman, and had a husband – with representations of flowers, would you,' said the gentleman. 'Why would you?'

'If you please, Sir, I am very fond of flowers,' returned the girl.

'And is that why you would put tables and chairs upon them, and have people walking over them in heavy boots?'

'It wouldn't hurt them, Sir. They wouldn't crush and wither, if you please, Sir. They would be pictures of what was very pretty and pleasant and I would fancy –'

'Ay, ay, ay! But you mustn't fancy,' cried the gentleman, quite elated by coming so happily to his point. 'That's it! You are never to fancy.'

'You are not, Cecilia Jupe,' Thomas Gradgrind solemnly repeated, 'to do anything of that kind.'

Dickens links these two types of learning with the respective family structures and home environments of Sissy Jupe and Thomas Gradgrind.

Learning in infancy

Psychoanalytic theory, and in particular the ideas of Melanie Klein and the post-Kleinians, places great importance on experiences in infancy for shaping how we subsequently learn. Waddell (1998) writes, 'A child's capacity to develop and grow internally is closely related to the kind of learning that has been going on from the earliest phases of his life.'

In her 1931 paper, 'A contribution to the theory of intellectual inhibition', Klein puts forward her idea that every child is born with a desire or instinct to find out about the world. She called this 'the epistemophilic instinct'. Initially, this curiosity centres on the mother (or primary caregiver) but gradually, as the child grows, it extends to other people in his immediate social sphere. In particular, the father, siblings, and the links between these people and the mother become the object of his interest. For this curiosity to continue to grow and to extend to a desire to learn and know about other things is dependent on a delicate interplay between the motivation behind the child's curiosity and the parents' emotional capacities.

Drawing on Klein's ideas, Bion (1962) has emphasized that the foundations for learning are established in the mother–infant relationship. As Waddell (1998) writes:

The dominant emphases of these modes may be significantly altered in the light of later experience, and in relation to a range of environmental factors, but important patterns are laid down in these early days, patterns which in simple terms may be defined as stemming from the nature and quality of the relationship between baby and carer.

(pp. 102–103)

So if a mother can be interested in what it is that is really making her baby cry, say, on this occasion, rather than quickly putting it down to wind, or tiredness, or teething, or hunger – and it may of course be any of these things – the baby has the experience of a person who really wants to find out the truth of a situation; who can remain interested in this particular baby at this particular moment. In this way, the baby begins to acquire a model of learning and is more likely to introject (take inside him) a figure interested in learning from experience.

The introjection of such a figure is not a straightforward equation. It does not necessarily follow that a baby who has a mother able to perform 'reverie', as Bion called this state of mind of helpful curiosity in the mother, will in turn become able to think about his own feeling states, be curious, etc. This is dependent also on the baby's disposition – whether he is able to tolerate frustration and gratefully take in what is given, or whether he feels so envious of his mother's abilities that he destroys them. However, this kind of experience is a good basis from which to start. If a baby has a mother who is unreceptive and unresponsive, he does not have the experience of someone grappling to understand his primitive, inchoate feeling states. In the absence of a containing presence, a baby may resort to expelling anxiety through projection and this may remain a dominant feature throughout development. Inadequate containment is bound to be the experience of all babies at some time – it is when there is a persistent lack of connection between mother and baby that the consequences for the subsequent ability to learn are likely to be interfered with. This is perhaps most clearly seen when there is parental mental illness, family trauma or where babies are severely neglected or abused.

A year seven boy, Michael, could never complete a piece of work – he would continuously rub out words, never satisfied with what he had written. Even when told that he had done good work, he would throw it away in disgust, insisting that it was rubbish. He frequently lost homework and books. Things he had learned and seemed to know would drop out of his mind when he was asked to recall them. It was for these reasons that this boy was referred for psychological help. It emerged that Michael's father had left his teenage mother during her pregnancy and, soon after the birth, his mother gave Michael up for adoption. Neither parent had any further contact and Michael was looked after by a series of foster carers before being adopted.

During the course of some therapeutic work, it became possible to understand that Michael's repeated experience of abandonment and loss had left him feeling that nobody really wanted him. He felt like rubbish to be thrown away. He confided that he felt sure that none of his past carers would remember anything about him. These feelings could be directly linked to his attitude to the school work which he would abandon, treat like rubbish or forget about.

Difficulties in learning or the setting up of particular modes of learning are therefore set in motion very early on. These models of learning are shaped both by the baby's nature and the mother's preferred mode of learning, and are a product of the meeting of the minds and personalities of baby and carer. Of course, the development of a model of learning is also dependent on two other important factors: the pattern of learning preferred in the whole family and the child's stage of development.

Learning in the family

In their paper 'Family patterns and cultural educability', Meltzer and Harris (1986) explore the relationship between various family and organisational functions and the preferred mode of learning that this creates in the children. While they make the point that 'character is deeply etched by the preferred modes of learning', they also emphasise that this is open to modification through contact with other figures outside the family such as teachers. School is thus an opportunity for coming into contact with something different – a chance to experience a new way of learning.

Central to psychoanalytic theory is the concept of how the family is represented in the individual's mind – that is to say, how the Oedipus complex has been negotiated. Freud (1909) most vividly describes a five-year-old boy's struggle with his curiosity about the relationship between his parents in the case of Little Hans. Little Hans wrestles with the recognition of his parents as a sexual couple and Freud describes the fantasies that he creates to evade knowing this as well as the means by which he comes to terms with it. Freud used this case to illustrate what he held to be a universal phenomenon in recognising a constellation of facts around the Oedipal situation – that is, that one's parents had intercourse to produce you, that there is a difference between the sexes and the generations, that parents have a relationship which excludes the child, and so on.

The acceptance or otherwise of these facts of life can have long-lasting consequences for the capacity to learn. While this is dependent on the personality of the child, recognition can be facilitated or impeded by parental attitudes. Some parents manage to introduce children to the reality of their ongoing sexual realtionship gently and with great sensitivity. Others may flaunt it in a way which overwhelms the child, or try to hide it away with some idea that the child must be protected.

Alex Coren (1997) writes, 'Our attitude to education is influenced by what it represents to us.' To this we might add that our attitude to education is also influenced by what it represents to our parents. The older we get, the more this influence is an internal one, but for small children the enthusiasm with which parents embrace education profoundly affects children's ability to enjoy and make good use of school.

Latency

The transition to primary school

A child may already have had some experience of being away from his parents with children of his own age through attending nursery. However, transition to school proper has connotations that give it a particular significance in the child's mind. Going to primary school carries with it an expectation of being a big boy or girl. Paradoxically, it is at this point that the boy or girl may feel most vulnerable and like a baby again.

In *The Emotional Experience of Learning and Teaching*, Salzberger-Wittenberg (1983) considers some of the fears that may get stirred up at any point of transition in someone's educational career, and makes the point that while these fears of feeling lost, or of not knowing anyone, for example, may be more obvious in a five year old, they remain, in some form, with us, ready to be resuscitated at any new change.

Corresponding to this move to primary school is generally a shift in a child's mode of functioning and way of relating to the world. This is characterised by a calmness which distinguishes childhood from babyhood and adolescence, and is why the term latency is applied to the period of a child's life between the ages of about five and eleven.

Learning in latency

Latency is a time of repression of instincts which allows for a period of stability in which learning can take place. Erikson (1965) called this 'the era of industry', and a substantial growth in cognitive and intellectual capacities takes place in these years. The space for this period of calm learning at school is created through the employment of certain defence mechanisms in latency children. Latency defences might be characterised as splitting – keeping good and bad experiences separate, so that one person, thing or idea is given all the good qualities and the other all the bad; obsessionality – a way of keeping tight control on the world by means of ritualised thoughts and actions; and repression – the means by which unpalatable thoughts, feelings and memories are kept out of conscious awareness. These mean that, generally speaking, children of this age have an oversimplified view of the world, and are not troubled by conflict or the extremes of feeling that are often so apparent in toddlers and adolescents. Thus, the repression of instincts and splitting up of experience have certain consequences for the personality and lead to the constriction of emotional life.

These defences serve a particular function in relation to learning at this time of life. They allow for the storing up of important knowledge about the world and how it works. It is the period for laying the bedrock of information needed for a different type of learning that takes place in adolescence. It is at this time that children learn all the basics of reading, writing and arithmetic. The type of learning that goes on in latency does have certain qualities. These are described by Meltzer (1973) in his paper, 'Pedagogic implications of structural psychosexual theory':

> The concept of knowledge is still formulated concretely as facts amassed and not as links, insights, understandings, points-of-views etc. It is at this level that a hunger for facts and information is seen to exist in the latency child, often to a degree not distinguishable from hoarding and miserliness in the more obsessional children, but even in the healthier children, the collecting tendency is clear.
>
> (pp. 158–159)

It is not uncommon for children of this age to have encyclopaedic knowledge of dinosaurs or footballers. This proclivity for a certain kind of learning can make teaching children of this age a pleasure, and indeed many children greatly enjoy primary school.

The desire to collect and conform is very marked in latency children. Each year brings with it a new craze or toy which everyone must have. This is, of course, well understood and exploited commercially. Latency also marks the beginnings of life outside the immediate family circle, and these toys, crazes and shared knowledge serve as the currency with which new peer relationships can be negotiated. Friends are bound together by a common interest or hobby. Swapping football stickers in the playground also functions as an arena in which the rules of negotiation, friendship, commerce, can be worked out.

Schools and friends mark the beginnings of life away from home. As Rustin and Rustin (1987) point out, the setting for children's literature at this age is often away from home, out of sight of the adults. In the *Narnia Chronicles* by C. S. Lewis for example, grown-ups are not allowed into the magical land of Narnia. Children begin to mark their existence away from the family by the use of school slang, but the fragility of this foray away from home is often revealed when children call their teacher 'mummy' by mistake. This struggle to integrate home and school life is one of the major themes of latency – especially the early period.

It is important to add at this point that not all children have the external circumstances that make for the quiet development we have been describing. Trauma, abuse, discord at home can easily intrude into the world of a latency child, upsetting the equilibrium needed at this stage of life. In this respect, the primary school environment can play a vital role in restoring the balance. It provides a structure of regularity and certainty which helps children focus their minds on the task of learning.

A seven-year-old girl, Liz, began to get into fights with her classmates. Unable to concentrate herself, she would deliberately disrupt other children, by poking them, pulling hair and constantly talking. At parents' evening, her mother told the teacher that her husband had decided to leave and that Liz had been very angry and upset by this. What Liz seemed to be trying to convey through her actions was that the separation of her parents was something with which she was very preoccupied and which constantly intruded into her mind. She was letting her classmates know what it felt like to be unable to settle to work because of constant interference from painful thoughts – communicated as pokes, tugged hair and verbal interruptions.

To lump together all children between the ages of five and eleven does not do justice to the huge differences between children beginning primary school and those leaving it. Children between five and seven are mainly concerned with leaving babyhood behind. Between eight and ten is middle childhood when a latency state of mind is most in evidence. Towards the end of this age range, children begin to approach puberty and the preoccupations that brings. However, what we have been describing does represent an important general phase in a child's life. A period of stability is vital preparation for the less tranquil waters of adolescence, and the next major transition point – the move to secondary school. If some solidity has been achieved before puberty, it strengthens the personality and allows for the more combative and tempestuous style of learning seen in teenagers.

Adolescence

An adolescent is seen as being in a place which is neither childhood nor adulthood; a kind of assault course with physical, psychological and emotional obstacles to be negotiated. Adolescents are generally seen as rebellious, turbulent and difficult to manage. They are disapproved of for their dress, their language, their music, their attitudes and their behaviour. They are also envied for their youth, their passion and for all the opportunities which are seen as available to them.

The kind of adolescence which young people now go through in western society is not the same as it was in Victorian times and certainly not the same as in many other societies, where the transition between childhood and adult life is marked by a ritual at a given point and where there is little or no choice about what adult life involves. In this society, where compulsory education goes on beyond puberty, where training and employment choices are many and varied, where unemployment is a reality for many and where the media and advertising tell us what is and is not important and desirable, the adolescent is faced with a very complex set of tasks. Externally, the world of the adolescent is, by its very nature, constantly changing. It is not even possible to describe it in its own language as the terminology will have changed before this book goes to press. What was once 'hip' or 'fab' was later 'wicked', 'cool', 'safe' or 'bad'. The opposite has been variously 'bogus', 'sad', 'lame', etc.

It is difficult to separate the internal tasks of adolescence from the external world which teenagers inhabit, but for the purposes of this chapter, we are focusing on adolescence as a stage in development, a series of internal changes which begin to take place at around the time when children move from primary to secondary education. There are no fixed ages for these developments and, as with infancy and latency, the process is never quite completed. Adolescent parts of the self remain within the adult personality.

Early adolescence

The beginning of adolescence marks the end of latency. Gone or much reduced will be the preoccupations of latency which are usually relatively unemotional, focusing as they do on the mastery of the external world. Adolescence is characterised by a renewal of passion and emotionality and as such, has much more in common with infancy and young childhood. It begins in response to hormonal changes. Bodily changes stir up psychic energy but psychological and emotional development do not proceed at the same pace as physical maturation. A thirteen-year-old girl may have suddenly become capable of bearing a child, but few would expect her to have the emotional maturity to cope with the experience. A fourteen-year-old boy could father a child but, in our society, for similar reasons, is expected *not* to do so. The young adolescent is beginning the process of loosening the ties with parents, home and family and is finding out about himself as an individual, a member of various groups and a potential adult. The process, if going well, will involve him in flexing his muscles within a containing framework. Like the toddler moving further and further away from his mother in the playroom but coming back to base from time to time to reassure himself, the young adolescent moves away from base a step at a time, secure in the knowledge that he can return there and find it intact.

It is never as easy a process as this sounds. Young teenagers begin their withdrawal from family life in a variety of ways but it usually involves conflict, worry and hurt. Teenagers question everything their parents say, or they simply don't listen to them. They stay up late and sleep in late. They talk on the telephone for hours to friends they have been with all day. They hate homework. They love loud music. They become faddy about food. They either don't wash at all, or they wash all the time. They will walk twenty miles to raise money for a favourite cause but insist on a lift to school. They do not want to eat with the family but they want to know that the meal is taking place as usual. They do not want to go on the family outing but are outraged if the parents suggest going somewhere without them. The list is endless and is full of conflict and rebellion. In psychoanalytic terms, splitting and projection are very much to the fore. It is a world of extremes. Opinions are strongly held and judgements are made on every aspect of life. People are seen as good or bad and there is little tolerance for the bad. Relationships with parents may suffer as the adolescent begins to act out, and the parents begin to feel they are walking a tightrope between allowing greater freedom and maintaining reasonable control. All the anxiety, doubt and caution are projected into parents (and often teachers) while the adolescent walks away with apparent confidence.

If adolescence sees a renewal of projection and splitting, it also sees a renewal of Oedipal confusion. As adolescents become aware of their own burgeoning sexuality, they become more aware of their parents as a sexual couple. For many, this is an uncomfortable revival of feelings of rivalry with one or other parent which then have to be defended against and denied. Teenagers whose parents actually separate during their adolescence may therefore be faced with very complicated feelings, often of guilt. It is, of course, often the case that the marriage has been destabilised, for the couple, by a child becoming an adolescent. Other rivalries may also be rekindled and open warfare between siblings is not uncommon. Twelve and thirteen year olds can become obsessed with equality and justice, turning the home into a courtroom.

Adolescents in groups

One of the glaring contradictions in this phase of development is the way in which adolescents value individuality and yet stick rigidly to the norms of their chosen group. They must belong and feel secure in that belonging, they must share values, tastes and aspirations with the rest of the group. This means they have to have the same clothes, the same music, the same language and, broadly, the same attitudes. Within the sameness of the group, individuals can experiment a little, projecting parts of themselves into others – the leader, the bold one, the disruptive one, the studious one, the sexually active one and so on. By lodging parts of themselves in others, they can remain in touch with those characteristics while trying out new and different ones. In early adolescence, the groups are more likely to be single sex and are usually fairly fluid. Members come and go and are sometimes cruelly ejected.

Later adolescence

Later in adolescence there is a shift of emphasis, although aspects of disaffection and rebellion against authority may endure. Just as there was a moving away from dependence on the family, there are now the beginnings of moving away from dependence on a homogeneous group. There is usually a shift from group life to couple life and, while these relationships may not actually be permanent, they are checked against some sort of idea of permanence. Adulthood begins to beckon and choices need to be made about future direction. Life is no longer mapped out by a mixture of family style and compulsory school attendance. Individuals really do make choices, and how ready a young person is to do so will depend on how much the adolescent tasks have been successfully negotiated and what has been introjected from the experience. Late adolescence may extend into an individual's twenties and beyond, or may be postponed, only to be picked up again at a later stage in life.

Learning in adolescence

Alex Coren (1997) makes the point that at secondary school transfer, the education system as it is currently organised runs contrary to what is happening internally. Just when young people are falling prey to the muddle and confusion of adolescence, they are expected to learn in a more organised and conformist way. They have to adhere to school rules, to tackle large amounts of homework, to prepare for exams and to think about the future. Pupils are expected to make choices according to interest and aptitude just at the point when they want to go wherever their friends go. It is difficult to choose ancient history if everyone else in the group is choosing art. Most adolescents would agree that school life is of central importance to them. However, it is important not because of work, but because it provides the venue for so much of the struggle to find one's place socially and emotionally. Just as at home, young adolescents need the safety of the structure of school (rules and routines) to provide a secure base for their excursions into uncharted waters. Their ambivalence about their parents is mirrored in their ambivalence about their teachers, who are variously idealised and denigrated. School rules, while much needed, may be mocked, challenged or ignored.

When a young person is intent on avoiding the tasks of adolescence, or is so immersed in them that there is no space for anything else, it is likely that learning (in the classroom) will be seriously inhibited. Mary, a sixteen-year-old girl in her GCSE year, became involved with a young man two years her senior, who worked at the local leisure centre. He had time on his hands and money in his pocket and she quickly found herself agreeing to go out with him when she knew she should have been studying. She dropped behind in her coursework, lied about it to her teachers, and became more and more evasive as the submission dates approached. When challenged, she was defiant and mocking of her hard-working peers. Her best friend, Suzanne, was horrified by Mary's behaviour. She was risking so much. What about their plans to go to college together? Unable to acknowledge that she, herself, was terrified at the very idea of a sexual relationship and was harbouring feelings of deep hurt at being 'put aside' in favour of a boyfriend, Suzanne became rejecting and judgemental. She buried herself in her own studies and worked for such long hours at night that her health began to suffer. Her teachers noticed that all the life had gone out of her work; she was writing screeds but it was dull and repetitive.

In this vignette of a shifting friendship, Mary takes all the risks while Suzanne plays it safe. Suzanne, we might say, clings to latency while projecting all her adolescent impulses into Mary. Mary projects all the conformity and predictability into Suzanne. Projection forms the basis for all kinds of dynamics in the classroom. In order to feel OK themselves, adolescents or groups of adolescents may put all their feelings of stupidity, inadequacy or sexual immaturity into others. Bullying and racism begin with projection. There may also be complicated dynamics in operation between teachers and pupils. Teachers, like parents, can feel very stirred up by being in the company of teenagers. They remind us of aspects of our own adolescence and may provoke enormous feelings of envy or rivalry. Teachers who are unaware of their own responses and who are not able to recognise splitting and projection may very easily find themselves in rivalrous confrontations. In schools, disruptive, acting-out teenagers have always been more of a worry than quiet, withdrawn pupils. When a fifteen-year-old boy or girl starts to challenge the teacher's authority, the school has a tendency to behave like a family under threat and to make desperate attempts to reassert itself. The school faces exactly the same dilemma as the family. The young person desperately needs containment but is intent on not accepting it on any terms.

Adolescent difficulties

Adolescence is, by its very nature, never a comfortable time. For some, however, it is not the creative struggle described in the foregoing paragraphs, but a time of public disgrace or private agony. Even those who appear to be 'sailing through' may be suffering internally as they struggle to make sense of what is happening to them physically, sexually, emotionally and socially. They may be riddled with doubts and fears about the apparently contradictory forces at work in their lives. Adolescent difficulties range from many forms of delinquent acting out to many forms of destructive turning in on the self. Whatever the behaviour or symptom, the difficulty arises out of an experience of being out of kilter with family and unsure of one's place in the wider world. Adolescents seek affirmation from the group. They measure themselves against what they see, or think they see, to be happening to their peers and try to adjust their own behaviour accordingly. If they cannot achieve that reassuring sameness, or later cannot achieve the necessary individuation to carry them into the adult world, they may seek to avoid the psychic pain in some way or another.

A desire to be an accepted member of a group can, of course, lead to all kinds of delinquent or destructive behaviour. The power of the pressure to conform by drinking, taking drugs, shoplifting, bunking off school and so on should not be underestimated. It is a very narrow line between wanting to be like one's more daring peers and not daring to gainsay them. Others may deal with their feelings of not keeping pace in adolescence by sticking to 'latency' activities. Becoming a computer expert is currently one avenue of escape. This is not to suggest that adolescence and computers are incompatible; merely that they provide a ready escape route for some individuals who will then need help to broaden the scope of their interests to include more contact with human beings.

Girls and boys are perhaps equally prone to becoming depressed about the way their lives are developing or not developing. Boys sometimes give voice to feeling frightened about their own physical strength and by the power of their sexual urges. They are worried about the damage they might do. Both boys and girls can feel precipitated into sexual activity before they are ready. Girls are perhaps most likely to turn in on themselves and engage in secret self-harm or misuse of food. Even these apparently private afflictions can become 'fashionable' and be used by groups as a badge of membership. Alternatively, someone who is seen as not coping may be further burdened by becoming the target of projections and the victim of bullying. Young people who are unsure of their sexuality can fall into a kind of no man's land where they feel alienated from their families and insecure in their peer group. Adolescents who are themselves struggling with sexuality project all their uncertainty and difference into others and can be unforgivingly homophobic. There is often also some considerable confusion for sexually-active adolescents, between sexual excitement and the kind of physical comfort and reassurance which their infantile selves still crave.

What, then, are the factors which make it possible for one teenager to struggle on through adolescence while another gets caught up in dangerous acting out or self-destructive withdrawal? There can be no immunisation against adolescent difficulties, but it is the premise of this chapter that an experience of containment in infancy and of facilitated learning and development in young childhood will equip the child to make good use of primary and secondary school and ultimately, to make the transition into adulthood. A child who has had the experience of moving out from a secure base (see Chapter 6) in early life is more likely to repeat the process in adolescence. Adolescence provides an opportunity for reworking the Oedipal situation. If psychic work has been done on this in early childhood, it will be a reworking and not an entirely new preoccupation. Similarly, splitting and projection may be an inevitable feature of adolescent functioning but the individual who has, at other times, been capable of more integrated responses will be less likely to be caught up in extremes of attitudes and behaviour.

Conclusion

Schools have a vital role to play in facilitating this working and reworking of developmental processes. The school has to find ways of ensuring that there is space for all of this, while not losing sight of the primary tasks of teaching and learning. Those who plan the curriculum have a part to play, as do those who establish the school routines and write the whole school policies. Most important are the teachers who are in minute-by-minute contact with the children and who offer a relationship within which children can grow, develop and learn. However, there will always be a small but significant number of children in every year whose ability to learn is hampered by emotional and psychological difficulties and who will need an opportunity to reflect on these within a safe and supportive relationship, set apart, though not split off, from the educational tasks of learning and teaching.

Clinical counselling may offer these children such a relationship and such an opportunity, outside the classroom but always firmly located within the educational context. In addition, counsellors may play a vital role in helping teachers, heads and managers to think about the complexities of classroom dynamics and the demands of the various adult roles in a school setting as well as the particular difficulties of individual pupils.

References

Bion, W. R. (1962) *Learning from Experience*, London: Heinemann.
Coren, A. (1997) *A Psychodynamic Approach to Education*, London: Sheldon Press.
Dickens, C. (1854) *Hard Times*, London: Penguin Classics.
Erikson, E. (1965) *Childhood and Society*, Harmondsworth: Penguin Books.
Freud, S. (1909) *Analysis of a Phobia in a Five-Year-Old Boy*, The Standard Edition Vol. XI, London: Hogarth Press.

Klein, M. (1931) 'A contribution to the theory of intellectual inhibition', in *Love, Guilt and Reparation and Other Works, 1921–1945*, London: Hogarth Press, 1985.

Meltzer, D. (1973) 'Pedagogic implications of structural psychosexual theory', in *Sexual States of Mind*, Strath Tay, Perthshire: Clunie Press.

Meltzer, D. and Harris, M. (1986) 'Family patterns and cultural educability', in D. Meltzer, *Studies in Extended Metapsychology*, Strath Tay, Perthshire: Clunie Press.

Rustin, M. and Rustin, M. (1987) *Narratives of Love and Loss. Studies in Modern Children's Fiction*, London: Verso.

Salzberger-Wittenberg, I., Henry, G. and Osborne, E. (1983) *The Emotional Experience of Learning and Teaching*, London: Routledge.

Waddell, M. (1998) *Inside Lives*, London: Duckworth.

Chapter 2

Creating a holding environment in an inner city school

Florence Heller

Introduction

After the family, school is the social institution which has the closest contact with children for most of their formative years. The primary and increasingly demanding purpose of a school is clearly educational. At the same time, schools are uniquely placed to observe their pupils, to recognise social and emotional difficulties and to address needs which are interfering with the learning process and could continue into adulthood. At the same time, schools are uniquely placed to observe their pupils, to recognise social and emotional difficulties and to address needs which are interfering with the learning process and could continue into adulthood. Realising the potential of this position is not at all simple. Emotional and social needs are essentially private, unclear even to the individual experiencing them, and at school they are often masked by misleading behaviour which may repel rather than attract help and understanding. The challenge is to produce conditions in which troubled pupils feel safe enough to reveal their needs and in which someone pays attention and responds appropriately.

My ideas on this subject were developed during nine years' experience of counselling in an inner city girls' secondary school, situated in an area where half the population lives in local authority housing, some of it definitely sub-standard, and where the population density and the rate of unemployment are among the highest in London. The school has a strong reputation for being well organised, innovative and caring, and teachers often stay there for many years.

In this chapter, I describe how I applied Winnicott's notion of a holding environment and his related theories about emotional development in infancy to the continuity of care given by such a school and by a counsellor working within it. To emphasise the intrinsic relevance of Winnicott's theories, I refer to the influential ideas of Robert Langs, who stresses the need for continual surveillance of the way in which the holding environment is maintained in therapy. Langs writes about adult patients and developed his methods in private practice and specialised clinics. Troubled pupils are not patients, have not attained adulthood, are usually trying, and often failing, to cope with very difficult life circumstances which impede their development. While Langs himself would probably see that his approach requires modification in school counselling, there is a danger that some practitioners may be persuaded to apply them without taking account of important contextual factors.

Theory: a Winnicottian perspective

The holding environment

Winnicott used the term holding environment to describe how the 'good enough' mother (Winnicott 1960b: 145), who does not have to be perfect, manages the day-to-day care of her baby. Although processes, for instance, feeding and sleeping, may seem purely physiological, they 'take place in a complex psychological field, determined by the awareness and the empathy of the mother' (Winnicott 1960b: 44). Ordinarily, the mother herself is 'held' by the immediate environment, principally the father and the family, and is 'good enough', but if this support is lacking, the infant's 'personality becomes built on the basis of reactions to environmental impingements' (Winnicott 1960b: 54). I take the term 'environmental impingement' to mean any interference with the mother's ability to hold, and it is particularly relevant in areas of high social need. If there is no privacy, if there is racial harassment, if the mother is unsupported, even abused by the father, if there are money worries at a basic level of survival, the child looks to the school for order, dependability and understanding. The pastoral care system tacitly recognises this but there is less acknowledgement that many subject teachers also symbolically 'hold' pupils in ways they themselves take for granted, by reliability, by encouragement, by the whole way they do their jobs.

The facilitating environment

Winnicott saw the holding environment, where the mother's adaptation to need is almost complete, becoming a facilitating environment. Here the infant becomes less dependent, capable of signalling wishes, not so reliant on the mother's 'almost magical understanding of need' (Winnicott 1960b: 50) and, through the mother's occasional failures to interpret signals properly, is exposed to the realities of human imperfection. Responding to new developments, the degree of the mother's adaptation gradually reduces, aiding a maturational process which represents the beginnings of eventual separation from her. Similarly, teachers and counsellors have to let go and not try to preserve a pupil's state of particular dependency on them.

Transitional experience and phenomena

Extending his environmental concepts, Winnicott postulates 'an intermediate area of experiencing, to which inner reality and external life both contribute' (Winnicott 1971a: 3). Play, the basis of 'the whole of man's experiential existence' (Winnicott 1971b: 75), and an endless variety of symbols – which he terms 'transitional phenomena' – including transitional objects, belong in this area. A bedtime story, a tune, a blanket or a toy may, for instance, be treasured by the infant, easing separation and defending against anxiety (Winnicott 1971a: 4). Winnicott says that the intermediate area, which has continuing significance for cultural life in adulthood, is highly variable, and clearly social and emotional deprivation restrict it.

Theory in context

A holding environment for school counselling

In school counselling, a holding environment is created by the management of boundaries, referred to in psychoanalysis as the 'ground rules', critically important in all psychotherapies. Marion Milner described the ground rules as a picture frame which sets off the therapeutic relationship from the rest of reality and so 'makes possible the full development of the creative illusion that analysts call transference' (Milner 1952: 183).

The notion of transference is central to psychoanalysis and all psychotherapeutic practioners, including school counsellors, need to be clear about it. Robert Langs sees transference as including 'all distorted and inappropriate responses and perceptions of the therapist' derived from the individual's feelings about experiences in his or her life (Langs 1979: 554). This kind of understanding increases awareness of the fact that a pupil's reactions to the counsellor and to teachers and the feelings the pupil arouses in them convey a lot about that pupil's other significant relationships, past and present.

Langs is a contemporary American psychoanalyst who has taken Milner's term 'frame' and drawn upon Winnicott's and Melanie Klein's theories to focus on the way in which the holding environment for therapy is managed. What he calls the 'fixed frame' includes the relatively unchangeable rules or boundaries like time, place and confidentiality and privacy, while the 'variable frame' refers to the therapist's relative anonymity and neutrality. Contending that 'the frame itself is the single most fundamental component of the analytic and therapeutic interactions' (Langs 1979: Preface), Langs says that deviations from it are frequent and often disregarded. He holds that frame management should be strictly maintained and monitored, constantly identifying and working with transference elements, and he claims that this is the most important area for therapy. The widening of the boundaries which is both necessary and helpful in multidisciplinary work would not fit into this model.

Clearly, good and reliable handling of the frame is critically important and Langs' analysis raises awareness of this, but, carried to extremes, the essence of Winnicott evaporates. If a mother constantly re-examined the way she managed her baby's care, her spontaneity and her sensitivity to its essential needs would surely be reduced. Similarly, if a school counsellor took Langs too literally, unrelenting concentration on the state of the relationship could reduce her receptivity to the varied needs which emerge within the frame, could baffle the pupil and conceivably invite charges that the counsellor was getting the relationship out of proportion.

The exclusivity which characterises Langs' view of the holding environment is at variance with Winnicott, whose concepts follow maturational development, expanding like living organisms. In the facilitating environment, the individual is not held so tightly and this allows for increasing independence and transitional experience. These notions are particularly important in the area of team work. Langs deplores deviations from the frame which occur in institutional settings but, taking a Winnicottian view, counselling in schools has its advantages. The confidence which teachers display when they refer pupils gives a solid basis to the establishment of trust, and colleagues inside, and sometimes outside, schools can support and complement the counselling. Both teachers and counsellors are facilitating healthy expansion into new relationships and further sources of help.

The following section gives three case studies, Marie, Lulu and Caroline, which show the counsellor working closely with particular teachers, sometimes using the frame and viewing the boundaries in ways which differ from traditional psychodynamic practice, certainly from Langs' approach. While most ground rules, like having regular sessions of fixed duration, were strictly maintained, the educational, institutional setting and the degree of emotional and social deprivation required certain adaptations which are consistent with Winnicott's theories. Thus the following themes are illustrated:

1   In secondary schools, pupils are in transition from childhood to adulthood. Therefore a counsellor sees those with unmet needs from childhood (Lulu) and those who, as emerging adults, are seeking understanding and insights (Marie and Caroline).
2   A school is not insulated from the wider environment. Any social deprivation characterising a given area has implications for teachers and for the counsellor who sometimes encounters needs which cannot be addressed by the relationship alone and require other interventions (Lulu).
3   In a school, collaboration between the counsellor and teachers is necessary and useful. Providing this happens with the participation of the pupil, processes which arise in counselling are extended and the creative coupling of teacher and counsellor can be therapeutic for pupils whose lives are often bereft of such models (Marie, Lulu and Caroline).

Clinical work

The counsellor combines with the art teacher: the case of Marie (fifteen)

Langs says that the ideal for therapy is 'a neutral location, a professional building and a private, unshared office' (Langs 1979: 6). The room allocated for counselling is, in contrast, undeniably part of the school, a fact which is bound to arouse anxieties, sometimes overt, sometimes covert. Marie, who was introduced by the deputy head after police had intercepted her nuisance calls to a pop star, questioned the location and contents of the room. A slight, pale girl of subdued but pleasant appearance, she assumed cool indifference but surreptitiously eyed me curiously. For thirteen sessions she talked incessantly about the world she imagined the pop star inhabited, stopping only to quiz me about the telephone and the filing cabinet. 'Is that where you keep that fat file on me?', 'I bet this room is bugged!' I realised that these preoccupations pertained to experience elsewhere, as yet unrevealed, and decided to reduce transference elements by confronting them at a reality level. Believing that there is a strong case for greater transparency, I opened the drawers to show her what was inside and invited her to read the brief factual record kept at the school. (Notes for supervision and my own deliberations were kept elsewhere.)

When Marie claimed she only came to see me to skip classes, I reminded her that she was making choices about her use of time, and noted that she was punctual and never left without making another appointment. Again, by means of these reality confrontations, scepticism was reduced, trust built up and she clearly felt more at ease. She now carefully removed her jacket whenever she entered the room, revealing underneath another torn jacket, richly adorned with safety pins, badges and buttons, and talked about herself instead of her idol. Her distinctly unusual, nomadic early childhood still mystified her, and a younger brother whom she hardly remembered had died in distressing circumstances. Her parents were now separated and she lived mainly with her mother, her mother's partner and their children in cramped conditions. They got on reasonably well (she described her mother as more like a sister) but she knew they were glad that she spent weekends with her father, a time she herself dreaded. Formerly a professional boxer, he collected old weapons and had an obsessive belief that he must stand guard over her, waiting at the school gates and questioning other girls about her. When I suggested that her apparently resigned attitude towards this violation of her privacy was belied by her earlier anxieties about the privacy of counselling, she saw the contradiction and was relieved to have her resentment out in the open. Previously uncommunicative and lacking friends, she gradually accepted the possibility of intimacy without betrayal, formed a friendship with another girl coming for counselling and began to 'fit in'.

Marie's favourite subject was definitely art and she loved fashion and design. When the class displayed their artwork I accepted her suggestion that I should look at it. Interestingly, this deliberate extension of the facilitating environment helped to validate her creativity and provided a link with her art teacher, who subsequently called to see me. She had taken a group to a gallery and Marie had behaved abominably, hiding and not keeping to arrangements. The teacher was exhausted and said that she would never take her out again. I sympathised, commented that it was only through school that her life could expand, cited the ever-vigilant father at the school gates and, of her own accord, the teacher realised why unwonted freedom had gone to Marie's head. No longer taking her behaviour personally, she deepened her interest and, through her special attention, provided the intermediate area of experience described by Winnicott. Marie's work developed surprisingly, her drawings, previously small and controlled, becoming large, imaginative and intriguing. Though major problems remained unresolved, she was now valued, respected and had opportunities for creativity.

Writers on adolescence recognise that the wish to find new relationships is counterbalanced by a deep need for privacy, and Marie exemplifies this paradox. Her preoccupation with the pop star was an escape from her restricted life and a substitute for real relationships, but also a defence against 'being found before being there to be found' (Winnicott 1963: 190). The sense of identity needs time to evolve and the delicacy of this process must be respected. There are reservations about accepting help, anxieties about losing control and understandable fears about consequences of confiding.

With Marie, as with all the girls whom I saw, the aim was to provide a holding and facilitating environment, where she would feel safe enough to reveal sensitive matters which concerned her and would be listened to and responded to appropriately. Awareness of transference factors increased understanding but were only occasionally made explicit and, when in Marie's case they were particularly strong, I made a calculated decision to reduce them by confronting her with realities which, as with the facilitating mother, can aid maturation if there is still a degree of protection. It was after this confrontation that she talked about herself and made friends.

The involvement with the art teacher which arose from Marie's initiative could be considered a deviation from the frame but it fits Winnicott's theories, extending the hold into the institution, facilitating moves towards independence, and increasing the transitional experience which was so important to her.

Collaborations

Whereas Marie's need for help was identified by an outside agency, both Lulu and Caroline first confided in approachable teachers who brought them for counselling. In such circumstances, a bond forms between pupil and teacher and referring her to someone else is an act of faith, sensed by the pupil. The teacher who brought Lulu always spent time on the referral process, sensitively explaining in the pupil's presence why she had suggested counselling. This provided a basis for the counselling itself and for future collaboration, if needed. Of course, the crucial issue of confidentiality arises in the area of collaboration, and its application in school counselling is considered after the cases of Lulu and Caroline.

The teacher brings in the counsellor: the case of Lulu (twelve)

Lulu was referred by the head of year, a very experienced teacher, alert to indications that pupils may have personal difficulties and need help. Lulu tried hard, had friends, was compliant and no problem in class, but the head of year and tutor noticed she was thin, often tired, pale and prone to day-dreaming. After a spate of lateness, the head of year spoke to her about their concern and Lulu acknowledged that she was very unhappy. She hated being late for school, which she saw as a haven from her troubles, but, like a number of others, she had work to do first, helping with younger siblings. At night there were more chores and no time to relax or play. When she welcomed the suggestion of counselling, the head of year brought her to me – a thin, serious little girl with large eyes and a cloud of dark hair, sheltering under the wing of her teacher.

During the first few weeks, it emerged that Lulu lived with her father, nearly seventy and no longer working, her stepmother, aged thirty-three, and their daughters, aged four and two. Her stepmother had been friendly with her natural mother who had a history of mental illness and who had been 'sleeping rough' for some years. Occasionally the natural mother visited them, and, looking very unkempt, had a bath, stayed overnight and then vanished again. Lulu's father had begun to object to these unpredictable visitations. Sometimes her mother telephoned to speak to Lulu or sent her a coin in an envelope. Lulu clung to these signs that her mother thought about her and, perhaps, even loved her.

Until her father began living with her stepmother, he had worked, leaving Lulu with a daily minder and looking after her himself at night. At that time, he and Lulu were closely bonded but Lulu now felt he had abandoned her, seeing her as a 'skivvy' to help him keep his new family together. Recently, her stepmother had left home for several weeks, and, since her return, demands on Lulu had increased. In the mornings, Lulu did her quota of household chores, arriving at school exhausted, often without breakfast. At night she looked after her sisters, sharing a bed with the younger, loving them and resenting them simultaneously. She had a rivalrous, hostile relationship with her stepmother, privately wishing she would leave for good.

Part of our agreement with Lulu when counselling began was that the head of year would see her father, whom she already knew, and discuss Lulu's needs. Before doing so, she arranged for the school doctor to see Lulu and consequently was able, in an unthreatening way, to alert her father to the fact that she was distinctly underweight. His earlier concern for Lulu was reactivated and he acknowledged that she bore the brunt of their overwhelming financial and other problems.

Lulu's stepmother was in care as a child, had a baby in her early teens who was adopted, and she and Lulu's father had no objection to renewed contact with social services. Concerned about all the children, social services provided extra resources on a preventive basis, the health visitor and general practitioner were consulted and a local church group, who had known them previously, offered play opportunities to the children. This carefully coordinated help was welcomed by the family, taking pressure off Lulu, who nevertheless continued in counselling for a year.

Lulu used her time with me in two main ways. Firstly, she continued to express her anxieties about her mother, for whom she felt responsible, longing to help and worrying about her in bed at night, especially in cold weather. Like her mother, she felt she was an outsider, adrift in the world. What would happen to her? Secondly, an equally important function of counselling was that of role fulfilment. Lulu had adult responsibilities too early and her life was bereft of play. She therefore used the play materials extensively and a significant result of our contact arose from the freshly picked flowers I kept on my desk. Noticing that they delighted her and that she was drawn to them, I suggested she should have them at the end of the day. On her own initiative, she began a collection of dried flowers which we then worked on together. Again on her own initiative, she moved on to make scrap-books from flower pictures which she cut out from magazines and catalogues. This sustained activity had a surprising outcome. Her stepmother, whose own childhood had seriously lacked opportunities for play and creativity, began to join in Lulu's activities, forming a new, totally unexpected bond between them.

My own role became less important and Lulu herself made the decision to stop counselling and concentrate more on school work, though occasionally calling in when she had something to report, like being made a monitor. She was no longer marginalised in the family and spent the rest of her schooling reasonably productively, with continuing encouragement from the teacher who referred her and who later taught her younger sisters.

The symptoms of tiredness, thinness, pallor, inattentiveness and lateness observed in the classroom had many possible, interrelated explanations – emotional, physical and environmental – and between them the teacher and the counsellor addressed all these areas of concern. The holding environment includes 'the total environmental provision' and when it transpired in counselling that Lulu was being deprived of child-hood, was hungry and lacked a holding environment, it was in keeping with Winnicott's notions to creatively use resources outside counselling.

The counselling relationship could nourish Lulu emotionally but not physically, and could not deal alone with unwitting neglect and exploitation. In any case, it is hard to separate emotional and social needs. Social deprivation arouses strong feelings in any individual, adult or child, who experiences it.

Giving the flowers to Lulu was consistent with Winnicott's emphasis on spontaneity, on play and transitional experience. Referring to a regressed patient in analysis, he distinguishes between wishes and needs (Winnicott 1954: 288) and this distinction is even clearer when one encounters real deprivation. It was not a case of gratifying wishes but an intuitive response to signs that she had basic needs as yet unfulfilled – needs which also existed within the immediate family circle. The beauty of it was that Lulu treated the flowers in such a way that they became transitional objects, which brought her closer to her stepmother and eased the separation from the counsellor which she herself initiated.

Counsellor and teachers form a protective alliance: the case of Caroline (fourteen)

Caroline was referred because she was a loner who sometimes burst into uncontrollable tears. Though teachers commented on her politeness, some complained about her stubbornness. For instance, she would refuse to complete her work, even when doing well, and she absolutely would not leave margins in her work.

Caroline was a large girl who, when her tutor brought her to see me, had an air of despondency relieved by flashes of sharp humour which suggested an alert intelligence. Both she and her tutor knew I would be leaving in six months and, though initially Caroline expressed relief that our involvement would be limited, a rapport was quickly established and the idea of my departure soon became hard for her to accept.

Whenever Caroline entered the room, she asked whether she could close the curtains ('sorry to be rude') and she regularly pretended to other pupils that she was attending a special class. When she talked about life at home, tears rolled down her cheeks, although she did not actually cry. It transpired that she was extremely isolated, having been left alone since early childhood while both parents worked long hours, paying off the house that was central to their existence. Religious pictures hung on the walls and Caroline felt that the eyes of the Virgin followed her everywhere. Though physically big and strong, she was nervous of both parents and believed they disliked her. 'I must admit I'm very disappointed in my parents. I thought they would have loved me, even spoilt me a little.'

She had three stepsisters, one by her mother, two by her father, all living away from home. She did not get on with them and said her mother's daughter gave her mother expensive presents which she gushed over, and 'I can't compete with that'. At school she had difficulty making friends, though others were apparently tolerant of her, and she distrusted adults. She saw herself as unlovable and twice referred to her 'blackness' as a barrier to forming relationships. In primary school, she once hit a teacher and she remained afraid of her own strength. Her politeness and formality seemed partly related to this as well as to parental training, but in counselling she soon spoke from the heart, expressing herself freely and graphically.

A session with Caroline

Caroline said immediately that things had gone badly since she last saw me. During the holiday, her cousin Cordelia came from Barbados and the family was 'all over her'. Her mother 'went on about Cordelia this and Cordelia that' and her stepsister had constantly visited, 'slagging me off' in front of their cousin – 'look at that fat ugly lump' and 'worse I wouldn't repeat'. I said I knew she had looked forward to her cousin's visit. Did she get to know her at all? No, she was definitely left out of everything.

Above all, she wanted to tell me about an incident with her mother. One evening, when Caroline was trying to do her homework, her mother was having a bath and kept asking Caroline to do things for her – bring her underwear, scrub her back and so on. (She once said her mother treated her as a slave.) Caroline had a bath after her mother and was washing herself when her mother burst in and began hitting her and trying to scratch her. Caroline cried and shouted 'Leave me alone!', dashing from one end of the bath to the other till her mother desisted. Later she asked, 'Why do you pick on me?' to which her mother replied, 'Because you're the youngest and the only one I can pick on.' I said this must have been most upsetting for her and asked whether anything similar had happened before. She said her parents did not usually knock her about, though sometimes she felt they were on the verge of doing so. When much younger, playing with her mother's makeup, she broke the box. Her mother flew at her, hit her again and again and tried to push something down her throat. Nothing like that had happened since but she still dreamed about it. I said it was clear that she felt very alone and unprotected and I hoped the school could find ways of supporting her. How would she feel about some direct contact with her mother and father, either by a teacher or a social worker? She said her tutor had suggested the same thing but she definitely did not want this as she would be severely punished. They would certainly stop her seeing me. I had to understand that, in their family, everyone was expected to know right from wrong. Talking about them at school would be unforgivable. She could not even keep a diary because her mother searched her room. Anyway, she needed a real person to listen to her. She had told two friends about coming to see me and they seemed to understand. I said this was a big step forward and that it was the first time she had spoken about having friends (she had earlier accepted my observation that she rebuffed friendly overtures although she desperately wanted them) and about confiding in her tutor, whom she had always liked but had previously hesitated to trust too much.

As our session concluded, I pointed out that in recent weeks she had raised matters we could not resolve alone. She had already spoken with her tutor. How would she feel about a special meeting with her? I was thinking, not only about the recent disturbing incident with her mother, but also about the fact that Caroline had destroyed a letter to her parents, asking them to collect a recent report, and she was now riddled with anxiety, wondering when the truth would out. Together we deliberated and decided to consult her tutor.

The subsequent joint session ultimately strengthened Caroline's relationship with the school. With regard to the confidences about her parents, she experienced our concern and our acknowledgement of her distress, trusting us when we said that we would not act precipitately and would always respect her feelings.

The undelivered letter was dealt with differently, beginning a problem-solving process which boosted Caroline's confidence in her abilities. She repeated what she had told me: that when her mother came to discuss her second year report she was disgusted with it, shouted at Caroline in the corridors and neither parent had ever let her forget it. Consequently, the next time Caroline assumed the report would be bad and disposed of the letter. Her tutor said that in fact this report was much better and suggested that the head of year should go through it with her before her parents saw it, a successful strategy as the head of year gave her a realistic and encouraging appraisal of her work. When her mother finally came in, she received a much more positive view of Caroline's performance.

The outcome was pleasing from several points of view. Caroline was ambitious and dreamed of becoming a lawyer, thus showing her family that they underestimated her. When she left work unfinished, it was because she was never satisfied. I hoped that her teachers' belief in her might help her do better and that her parents' attitude might soften a little. Certainly she was closer to two key teachers, who were aware of her vulnerability.

This was important to Caroline, to the tutor and to me. I would like to have seen her for longer and, particularly as my replacement was uncertain, I had realised early on that the holding environment she so badly needed had to be maintained and widened. Cases like Caroline's, where pupils appear to be in unsympathetic, even hostile environments, are anxiety provoking, and the involvement of a more senior teacher, in a position to share responsibility with the tutor on a preventive and protective level, was very welcome.

Confidentiality and collaboration

Langs says that confidentiality is among the most important of the ground rules, and yet issues and infringements arise very frequently these days. Certainly in work with children and young people, confidentiality has become harder to define and convey in absolute terms. Case studies given here show that needs revealed within the frame sometimes bear directly on classroom behaviour and on a pupil's well-being, even safety. While not for a minute suggesting that a counsellor should talk loosely about revelations in counselling, I maintain that, if the counsellor and the pupil agree that it is in the pupil's interests to seek other sources of help, sharing strictly relevant information, this is in keeping with the facilitating environment and can help significantly.

Confidentiality has been defined as 'an intimacy of knowledge, shared by a few who do not divulge it to others. . . . It is a contract of trust' (Reber 1985: 146). This fits the collaboration which occurred with Marie, Lulu and Caroline, where the coupling of counsellor and teacher gave them experience of holding and facilitating environments and transitional experience which their lives had lacked. One thing is certain – that in a school, a counsellor's reputation in such matters is built up over time, by what she does rather than by what she says she will do. When I left, although Caroline still had periods of depression and tearfulness when she would reach out for help, she was more integrated in her tutor group, more trusting with her teachers and more persevering with her work.

Conclusion

> There are many varieties of psychotherapy and these should depend for their existence, not on the views of the practitioner but on the needs of the patient or of the case.
>
> (Winnicott 1961: 232)

In this chapter, I have stressed the significance of the school as a place where not only educational but also emotional and social needs can be recognised and at least partially addressed. I have suggested that Winnicott's own notions of the holding, and later the transitional environments, can increase understanding of these wide-ranging needs and allow for the collaborative work which is necessary and useful. Describing how the holding environment is created, I have drawn on the writings of Robert Langs and, without discounting the value of his contribution, have argued that a strict application of his views on frame management (particularly the rules of confidentiality), though probably perfectly appropriate in private work with adults, in the context of schools would isolate counselling, and therefore pupils, from other valuable sources of help.

The ideas I have put forward are based on long experience in areas of social and economic deprivation, firstly in family casework and secondly in school counselling, where I constantly noted the close interrelationship between educational, social and emotional factors and realised that whenever this interrelationship was significant, only a multidisciplinary approach was truly effective. Having previously worked with schools from outside I found it very beneficial to work from inside, and I hope that the case examples given convey the fact that counselling can be enriched (as with Marie) and supported and extended (as with Lulu and Caroline) by close collaboration with committed colleagues.

I was fortunate in the school I worked in but, even there, some teachers were obviously much more in touch with emotional and social needs than others and usually they were the ones who sought my help. In the limited time available I concentrated on the strengths in the girls themselves, in the teachers with whom I worked, in the school as a whole and in the community.

A recent report compiled from data collected over three years from *The Annual Health Survey for England* shows a clear correlation between low income and emotional and behavioural problems. In the lowest income group, 20 per cent of boys and 15 per cent of girls had behavioural and emotional difficulties, whereas in income groups over £24,380, the proportion was approximately 6 per cent of boys and 4 per cent of girls (Primatesta and Prescott Clark 1998). These dramatic findings will not surprise teachers in inner city schools who have always known that many of their pupils are held back educationally by their reactions to very adverse life circumstances. Obviously this daunting situation must be addressed at many levels, but the findings provide a strong argument for the availability of counselling which works in ways contingent upon the actual context and which increases the holding capacities of the school itself.

References

Langs, R. (1979) *The Therapeutic Environment*, New York: Jason Aronson.

Milner, M. (1952) 'Aspects of symbolism in comprehension of the not-self', *International Journal of Psycho-analysis*, 33: 181–195.

Primatesta, P. and Prescott Clark, P. (eds) (1998) *Health Service for England 1995–97*, London: Department of Health.

Reber, A. S. (1985) *The Penguin Dictionary of Psychology*, Harmondsworth, Middlesex: Penguin Books.

Winnicott, D. W. (1954) 'Metapsychological and clinical aspects of regression within the psycho-analytical set-up', in *Through Paediatrics to Psychoanalysis*, London: Hogarth Press, 1975.

—— (1960a) 'Ego distortion in terms of true and false self', in *The Maturational Processes and the Facilitating Environment*, London: The Hogarth Press and The Institute of Psycho-analysis, 1965.

—— (1960b) 'The theory of the parent–infant relationship', in *The Maturational Processes and the Facilitating Environment*, London: The Hogarth Press and The Institute of Psycho-analysis, 1965.

—— (1961) 'Varieties of psychotherapy', in *Deprivation and Delinquency*, London: Tavistock Publications, 1984.

—— (1963) 'Communicating and not communicating, leading to a study of certain opposites', in *The Maturational Processes and the Facilitating Environment*, London: The Hogarth Press and The Institute of Psycho-analysis, 1965.

—— (1971a) 'Transitional objects and transitional phenomena', in *Playing and Reality*, London: Tavistock Publications.

—— (1971b) 'Playing: the search for the self', in *Playing and Reality*, London: Tavistock Publications.

Chapter 3

Intimacy and distance

Working with students with disabilities in a residential setting

Miranda Ommanney and Jan Symes

Introduction

This chapter focuses on therapeutic work in a special residential school and further education college for students from seven to twenty-two years of age. All students have profound physical disabilities. Some disabilities are genetic in origin, some result from trauma at birth, some have been acquired at a later stage. Often students have severely reduced life expectancy with some disorders causing gradual physical and/or intellectual deterioration. Intellectual range is wide, however – from severe learning difficulty to university entrance. Many have impaired speech, sight or hearing and the means by which they communicate is varied and may include augmented communication.

An eclectic counselling team, embracing a range of approaches including person-centred, psychodynamic and expressive therapies, includes a chaplain and social worker. Counsellors work with individuals and groups, groupwork usually being themed to specific issues such as leaving college, bullying, or living with muscular dystrophy. In addition, staff support and training are offered to encourage psychological awareness among carers and teachers.

When working with students, various therapy techniques are utilised as appropriate to student age and cognitive ability. Art and sand tray therapy (Dundas 1978) are often helpful in work with younger students, and counsellors are constantly challenged to find ways to overcome communication difficulties. This chapter, however, focuses on a single person-centred counsellor's work[1] with individual students. The focus will not only be on the process of this work but on the impact of working in the context of this particular client group in this particular setting.

Theory

The person-centred approach

Person-centred counsellors start from the assumption that each individual has within them a 'self-actualizing tendency': 'the capacity . . . latent if not evident, to move forward toward maturity.' What is needed is a 'suitable psychological climate' for this 'tendency' to be released. Released, the tendency 'becomes actual rather than potential' (Rogers 1967: 35). For the person-centred counsellor, the 'suitable psychological climate' is encapsulated in the term 'core conditions'. These are the conditions of 'empathy', 'unconditional positive regard' and 'congruence' which the counsellor must be able to offer the client, if the healing power of the therapeutic relationship is to be effective and change enabled (ibid.).

The first of these core conditions, empathy, requires the counsellor to learn to see the world through the client's eyes, suspending their own perception. It also means engaging emotionally so as to recognise in themselves the feelings described by a client, while retaining an awareness of their own separateness. This enables them to travel side by side with the client through their emotional landscape.

Unconditional positive regard, or non-judgemental acceptance implies a valuing of the client as a person without imposing external conditions of worth. It allows clients to see themselves in a new light and to value themselves. It also allows them to see themselves as separate from their behaviours and circumstances.

Congruence demands that counsellors be real with clients. It requires a level of self-acceptance in practitioners which, when presented authentically, enables clients to be more open. It is about responding in a relationship as one human being to another, without roles or facades, allowing clients to drop pretences and defences and develop a healthy self-regard.

Theory in context

Counselling young people with disabilities

It could be said that humanistic counselling has, in its core philosophy, a strong anti-discriminatory stance which is particularly appropriate when working with clients with disabilities. Thus the counsellor aims to be alongside the client rather than being an aloof expert, as is commonly the case if using the 'medical model' of understanding disability (Matkin

1995). Yet any practitioner whose counselling philosophy lays emphasis on the core conditions can face serious doubts about their ability to offer those conditions to this client group. For example, how can a counsellor empathise with a person whose experience of life is so seemingly different from her own? The history of segregation of pupils with disabilities into separate schools has meant that many adults have not met or worked with people with disabilities (Reiser and Mason 1990). The resulting lack of awareness increases the chance of prejudice and preconceptions. Can we imagine what it is like to be in pain all the time, to be unable to walk, or talk, or go to the toilet unaided?

It is similarly difficult to offer non-judgemental acceptance. On meeting these students, many can wish that they were different: not disabled, not so cut off from normal human contact, not so limited in their expectations of life. Perhaps one of the most crucial elements in the personal growth of counsellors in this setting is learning to accept those things that cannot be changed, and, as their clients do, to work through them and around them. Thus counsellors need to address their own possible preconceptions so that they do not have a sense of pity or tragedy about these students.

In working with this client group, the third of the core conditions, congruence, can be the most troublesome. Student life stories are frequently traumatic and sometimes shocking. Can it possibly be helpful if their counsellors are visibly shocked by their predicament? And if counsellors have to hide their feelings, especially those of deep grief which often arise here, how can they find a way of working effectively that fits with their understanding of the therapeutic relationship? It is often a struggle to be open and honest with any client, but in these circumstances the dilemma is more complicated than usual. In attempting to respond honestly, might not a counsellor only succeed in helping the client feel worse? These justifiable anxieties undoubtedly colour the lives and work of the team and make each fresh encounter with a client a challenge to personal and professional integrity.

The team works with the knowledge that a small number of students can be expected to die during any school year. Others will deteriorate either physically or mentally or both. Some students will face major surgery on which their lives, or at least their future mobility, may depend. They may spend months in hospital and further weeks in the 'Medical Centre' at school, an experience they may well have to repeat many times in their lives.

The death of children is one of the most unacceptable facts of life, as is the thought of people in pain who cannot be made better. It is not surprising, therefore, that practitioners' anxieties often centre on what effect this work might have on them, and whether they will be strong enough to cope with it. They may also struggle with a recurring sense of inadequacy in the face of so much need (Menzies-Lyth 1988). Counselling young people with severe disabilities therefore raises questions about the counsellors' ability to maintain a professional relationship. The counsellor is called upon to hold, empathically, congruently and non-judgementally, immense pain and to refrain from giving way to their own desperate desire to 'make life better' for their clients. The struggle is to maintain therapeutic distance within an intimate healing relationship, rather than increase over-protectiveness and thereby block the clients' growth.

Family matters

Interestingly, disability itself is rarely a presenting issue. The majority of students have been disabled from birth or early childhood and, by the time they come for counselling, they are often very matter-of-fact about their physical condition and concerned about issues familiar to any school or college counsellor: family breakdown, conflict with parents or peers, self-esteem, etc. All these issues, however, are inevitably affected by the fact that they are disabled. Counsellors, therefore, must not pretend they do not notice the client's impairment but neither must they assume that the disability *is* the problem (Lenny 1990).

A high proportion of students live in single-parent or stepfamilies. Many of them believe that they were the main cause of their parents' broken relationship. Although this is a common belief among children of divorced couples, the disability of the child and its attendant stresses does put an enormous strain on the family and, where there is insufficient support, families do frequently break down (Murgatroyd and Woolfe 1982). Our clients therefore not only have to bear the loss and insecurity that follows a divorce but also a sense of responsibility for it that is even more acute than that of their non-disabled peers.

Parental over-protectiveness is another major difficulty facing these students. It is a familiar problem for teenagers everywhere – 'they treat me like a child', 'they won't let me stay out after 10.30' – but for these students, the frustrations are hugely magnified. It is not unusual for an eighteen year old to be fighting for the right to choose what clothes to put on and to get washed and dressed in privacy. The personal boundaries that need to be negotiated by any adolescent are thus far more difficult for a disabled teenager to establish. From handling their own finances, planning independent holidays and, ultimately, leaving home, to minor rights like making private telephone calls or choosing to have their ears pierced, every independent step can be delayed or blocked by anxious parents who cannot let go of the need to be needed, and to organise their child's life.

Parents are often weighed down by guilt and fear as well as love for their child, and demonstrate this by trying to do everything for them. They are often frightened to let them out of their sight, as if they are trying somehow to lessen the danger of further 'damage'. This is understandable, but maddening for the child. It can be very hard for him to confront his parents, or cope with having angry feelings towards them, when he is painfully aware of his need for their care, and often feels himself to be a burden. All these conflicting feelings – the young person's dependent needs uncomfortably coupled with a desire for independence, the strain on the adult carer's resources combined with the urge to protect and provide more – are central issues in counselling.

School and college matters

Students who are struggling with these kinds of difficulties can build up an enormous backlog of unexpressed socially unacceptable emotions such as anger, sadness, loss. Their inability to express them can be compounded by the prevailing atmosphere in school and college, where, as in many institutions, carers tend to cope with their own multi-faceted responses to their charges' predicament by keeping things light and jokey. In many ways, this can serve an excellent purpose as a defusing mechanism and everyone enjoys themselves all the more for it; but for someone full of grief, anger, guilt and fear, it only presents a further barrier to expressing these feelings.

There seems to be an institutional need to deny the existence of extreme pain, especially when the institution can offer no solution to it. Students may thus resort to 'acting out'[2] (Freud 1968) the feelings, using difficult, violent or otherwise antisocial behaviour, or self-harm. A smiling, cheery girl may be cutting herself at night to relieve the built up pressure of 'bad' feelings which have to be repressed all day. A confident, carefree-looking student may drink himself into oblivion on a regular basis as a relatively acceptable way of masking his despair. In giving students a safe place with permission to say how bad they feel, counsellors can help to ease this situation.

Clients are often terrified of being overwhelmed by bad feelings, of losing control or 'going mad', and may seek help in the hope that they can learn how to cover up these feelings more effectively. It can be very slow work to enable them to express their grief and fear a little bit at a time and help them to accept themselves as people with many emotions.

Referral, confidentiality and boundary issues

Society doesn't generally expect much of those with impairments. Their limitations are highlighted and their abilities not seen. They may not be offered the same resources as their able-bodied peers. Some families and professionals assume that students with learning disabilities will not be able to make enough sense of counselling for it to be useful. This is gradually being challenged, and the principle of equal access to services should improve access to counselling (Moulster 1998).

An aspect of working with this particular client group, in a residential setting alongside other multidisciplinary professionals, is that clients are often referred by staff rather than referring themselves. The counselling team may be contacted by care managers, unit leaders, teachers, occupational therapists, physiotherapists, GPs or even parents, asking us to see a student for a variety of reasons. Sometimes it is simply a case of someone close to the student becoming concerned that they are upset or depressed: they will usually discuss the idea of counselling with the student and obtain his agreement to the referral being made. This broad-based referral system can work very well, though some referrals seem to reflect over-protectiveness in the staff and an unhelpful tendency to make decisions on behalf of the students. An initial assessment session is used to filter out the student's wishes and needs from those of the referral source.

In some cases, however, the request for counselling comes as a result of unacceptable behaviour, and the student's agreement may not have been sought. The client in this situation may see counselling as part of a disciplinary process, and trying to establish a relationship of trust is likely to be difficult work. Even when agreement has been obtained, it may be of doubtful value because students may not realise that they really do have a choice. They are much more likely to say 'Yes' than 'No', especially if this seems to be the answer that will please. These uncertainties need to be explored early on, otherwise the work may be dogged by misunderstanding, reluctance and resentment.

Linked with client ownership of the counselling is the issue of confidentiality – who knows that a student is receiving counselling and who needs to know (Hamilton and Hopegood). The counselling team circulates a list of all its clients to a select number of staff members who are deemed to 'need to know'. Particularly at the school, where students' ages range from seven to sixteen, it is necessary for a few key people to know where each student should be at any time to ensure their safety. If a client fails to appear for counselling, the counsellor must inform the appropriate person so that his whereabouts and safety can be checked. This need has to take priority over confidentiality and counsellors have to accept this modification of their boundaries that the context demands (McGowan 1998).

The whole question of non-attendance needs to be treated with greater flexibility than in most other settings. A basic verbal contract in which client and counsellor commit to punctuality and regular attendance is the usual starting point, with an agreed method of advance warning in case of enforced absence. Breaking the contract is treated seriously and discussed, with a specified number of missed sessions leading to an end to the counselling. As in any counselling work, these boundaries are vital and add to the client's respect for the counsellor, himself and the work in hand. However, for some clients, remembering the time of a weekly appointment is a real problem. Some will solve it by keeping a written record in a safe place, but others will forget where the safe place is. If it becomes clear that there is a memory problem rather than a reluctance issue or a power game, it may be necessary for someone to remind the client each week, which means yet another person knowing about the counselling.

The age group of our clients, their lack of experience of boundaries and confidentiality, together with their varying levels of cognitive development, all complicate the manner with which we have to deal with referrals, confidentiality and boundaries. For example, for many, the fact that they have a counsellor is a matter of pride, and they will greet us enthusiastically in front of their friends if we meet accidentally. They will sometimes tell teachers or friends what they are working on in counselling, how they feel about counselling and even what they have been 'told to do'.

Telling clients what to do is not a characteristic of person-centred counselling (Mearns and Thorne 1988). However, it does highlight once again a problem deeply ingrained in working with this client group; namely, their ambivalent feelings about dependence and about the desirable nature of the capacity to choose. This ambivalence is particularly difficult for the older adolescents. Thus, though some of these boundary issues may seem minor, each small reduction in confidentiality and privacy is a reduction in potential empowerment and therefore needs careful consideration. Certainly, it is often true that 'the client doesn't mind', but in this situation that cannot be a valid guide. These clients need their right to privacy to be protected all the more vigilantly because they are often unable to claim it for themselves. They may want to keep some things private, but may not feel comfortable about claiming that right. Once again, it is a matter of recognising their capacity and asserting their right to choose.

Many of our students, aware of their need to become more assertive, more or less actively seek our encouragement. Others, however, are far more tentative, and we have come to recognise the importance of subduing our desire to push them towards a more assertive independence and, instead, wait unconditionally for such a time when they may be ready to see this need for themselves.

Clinical work

James

Choosing to engage

James is a client who was 'sent' for counselling because of his violent behaviour. I was told he had agreed to see me and felt positive about the idea. At our first meeting, however, he told me he didn't remember being asked, and wasn't too keen because he'd seen a counsellor at his last school and it 'didn't work'. Despite this, he agreed to stay and talk to me for the remainder of the session and then decide whether or not he would like to work with me. I explained that this was a choice I normally offered any new client and that he really could make up his own mind whether he wanted to come back next week. He seemed very unsure whether to believe me and then asked what I wanted him to talk about. When I said he could choose anything he liked, he was clearly surprised. He said he thought he'd been sent to me to talk about hitting people. I told him it was fine to talk about that if he wanted to, but he could choose something else if he preferred. Again he seemed rather suspicious and I could see that all this choice was making him uncomfortable. It wasn't what he was used to.

The issue of engagement is an important one, especially when working with young people. Students seem to make a quick assessment of adults and not wait if their initial impression is disappointment (Geldard and Geldard 1999). Anxieties and suspicions like James' are frequent at the beginning of counselling. They bring immediately to the fore issues of dependency, ownership, compliance and choice. With James, the unexpectedness of being given free rein was compounded by his low cognitive ability and high level of confusion about many areas of his life. However, if I hadn't waited for him to focus on something of his own choosing, I doubt if we would have made any headway. Eventually, he asked whether he should talk about his family. Silently, I wondered whether that was what his previous counsellor had suggested but soon felt ashamed of my cynicism. His family was exactly what he needed to talk about.

He began by telling me he wanted to 'sort them out', and for a moment I thought we were back with hitting people. But no, he wanted to sort out who was who and what belonged where. He literally couldn't tell me who was part of his 'real' family and who belonged to his foster family. He didn't know how many mothers, fathers or brothers he had.

During that first session, we only had time to 'sort out' the bare bones of what he knew and didn't know. One particular worry for him was whether the other, younger boys in his foster family were his own brothers or the children of his foster-mother. His only clear memory of his real mother and father was of being taken away from them in a police car with a flashing blue light. He thought he must have been about five at the time.

By the end of this first session, he was keen to come back and talk some more. However, during the next session he quickly exhausted his fund of knowledge about his muddled family. He couldn't remember anything else that might make things clearer. My own fantasies about the possible reasons for his removal from his parents suggested to me that he might have had good reason not to remember. If the police had been involved in such a dramatic way it seemed likely that James had been in real danger; perhaps abused, hurt or neglected. Memories of such experiences may well have been deeply buried.

We drew a diagram of what he'd come up with so far but it was full of question marks. He became upset and quickly shifted to being angry. I suddenly became aware of how big and strong he was, and how threatening he felt. He was showing me with the utmost clarity how his confusion led to violence (Casement 1985). When I empathically reflected that back to him, he seemed to recognise it and calmed down. We were able to talk about other times when that had happened, and at one point he smiled and said I'd managed to make him talk about hitting people after all!

A boundary issue: the need for flexibility

James' desperate desire to know the facts about his family presented me with a dilemma. Although seventeen, his emotional development and cognitive ability lagged several years behind and he was used to being treated as a child. He had asked his foster-mother about his family and she had said she couldn't tell him. He knew of no other source of this knowledge and repeatedly asked me if I could find out for him. I knew I probably could find out at least some of the answers, simply by asking his care manager, but that is not the kind of thing I usually do: not working strictly with what the client brings; not very person-centred. It is also, of course, a request to step over a boundary, to adopt more responsibility and to offer a different intimacy than the counselling relationship normally allows.

I suggested to James that he might ask his care manager himself, but two sessions later, he still hadn't managed to find anything out. I couldn't tell whether he was just too nervous to ask or hadn't been able to make himself clear. His distress was increasing, and I felt guilty at having seemingly made things worse for him. I felt that by encouraging him to think about his confusion and suggesting that others knew the answers which he was unable to find I had caused him additional pain. In the end, I asked the care manager myself.

In making this move, I clearly overstepped my usual boundaries, and the reasons for doing so took me right to the heart of a central difficulty in working with such clients. Essentially, I felt convinced that, by empathically recognising the real limitations of my client, my actions provided him with the real and symbolic resources he needed to 'sort things out'. Certainly, as a result of my discussion with the care manager and the information acquired, James gained relief and was able joyfully to claim two brothers. He continued to come to counselling for several more sessions and we talked about what it was like not to know or understand. James discovered that he could find out the answers to some things but not others, and established a goal for himself of asking questions before lashing out. While I feel there was a sense of progress here, I wonder if guilt was also a motivating factor in taking the action I did. Acknowledging this means that I may have acted out of *my* need more than his and, in doing so, may have missed an opportunity for fostering in him a deeper sense of empowerment, of independence, of the capacity to believe in his own ability to make a choice.

It is also important to be aware of the impact of the residual ethos of the institution on all the relationships between students and staff (including counsellors). The legacy of Victorian paternalism which invites collusion with the assumption that able-bodied adults are needed to get things done is one about which the counsellor needs to be constantly vigilant. We need to explore in our own personal development what brings us to work with such a stigmatised client group, and retain an awareness of how our needs affect our response to clients.

Another boundary issue: the need for firmness

Another dilemma James presented me with concerned his behaviour. It was no surprise to me that he didn't suddenly stop hitting people. I knew the reasons for his referral, and several key people in James' college life knew he had been referred for counselling. One of them sent me a note after a few weeks, mentioning two violent episodes. I wasn't sure why I was being informed or whether I wanted to be. My understanding was that the referral had been made because James' behaviour was seen as a symptom of his internal difficulties, and counselling was chosen as a way of helping him to address them. I generally experience the college as very enlightened about the causes of 'bad behaviour', and offering a high degree of tolerance and understanding of students who express their emotions in this way. However, I could also imagine that some members of staff might have been keen to have James 'sorted out'.

The counselling team holds weekly meetings offering an opportunity to discuss such matters, and I brought up my uncertainty and anxiety about James. I realised that I needed to be reassured that no one in the team or college was demanding that I 'cure' him of his violence, however welcome that outcome would be. After discussion, the team decided to formally discourage the sending of 'bad behaviour' reports on clients to their counsellors, and to secure management's agreement that there was no onus on us to respond to any that might be sent (Earwaker 1992).

Having said this, the outcome for James was that his violent episodes reduced in frequency and he seemed more settled. When our sessions came to an end, he told me he was 'better', and I later heard by chance that James was no longer causing so much havoc. I could have asked how he was getting on, and it is often very tempting to check up on the progress of ex-clients when they are still in college. It is much harder to 'let go' of clients when there is the constant possibility of meeting them in the corridor or hearing about them from others.

Jenny

Jenny was referred for counselling by her unit leader because she was becoming distressed about a close friendship. The unit leader had come to feel very powerless to help after weeks of trying to listen sympathetically and supportively (Mawson 1994). There was also a worry about a forthcoming operation to straighten Jenny's spine.

As soon as I met Jenny, I was aware of feeling protective about her. She was small and delicate-looking, softly spoken and very polite. At our first session, she was also in considerable pain. Her distorted spine prevented her from sitting up in her wheelchair, a fact which she seemed to accept with resigned stoicism.

The two elements that I had already been told about were quite distinct in her mind and she began with the operation. She was born with spina bifida but had been able to walk and run until she was ten years old. At that point she began to lose function in her legs, but was offered an operation to restore it. The operation failed, and after almost a year in hospital she went home with a wheelchair. By this stage in the story, I was feeling upset and angry at the unfairness and disappointment of this. Jenny, however, calmly and articulately continued her factual account.

Her need to use a wheelchair meant that she had had to leave her local school and circle of friends and become a boarder with us, two hours' drive away from home. She had been very lonely and homesick at first, partly because she was entering a group who had already established friendships and she was very shy. She felt she had eventually settled reasonably well but gradually began to find it more and more difficult to sit straight. Her spine was becoming twisted, constricting her breathing, and she had just been told that she would need a life-saving operation to insert steel rods alongside her spine to straighten her posture. The procedure was complicated by several factors: first, she still had some feeling in her legs and she had never given up hope that she might walk again. (The operation would almost certainly remove that possibility.) Second, the protrusion at the base of her spine, associated with spina bifida, was contributing to her inability to sit properly, but she had been told that its removal carried a risk of brain damage. Her surgeon had apparently admitted that the operation was risky and might not be successful. There was no other option but to attempt it, because without it she would not survive.

Jenny was still very calm while telling me this, while I felt more and more horrified. Like her unit leader, I was already almost overwhelmed with helplessness and could do no more than reflect back to her that she seemed very calm. She told me that there was no point in getting upset as there was nothing she could do about it and she didn't want to worry her family. It seemed that I was feeling the helplessness for her while she kept it buried. I wasn't sure I dared help her to dig it up, since I was having trouble keeping my own equilibrium as it was.

Jenny then moved straight to her other issue. She had made a best friend called Jane, a very big, powerful girl who ruled a group of her peers with a mixture of bullying and blackmail. This is how Jenny described her. When I said it didn't sound as if she liked Jane very much, she said she sometimes liked her and sometimes felt frightened of her, but she needed to stay friends with her because she wasn't close to anyone else. The other members of the group tolerated Jenny, and even showed her some respect, but only because she was Jane's friend. However, she was finding that to stay friends with Jane she had to do her bidding, which often meant being nasty to weaker students, and she didn't want to become a bully herself.

This is another familiar situation in institutions, where a 'pecking order' frequently develops. To be accepted by others, students have to fit in with the order wherever they can, and, like Jenny, may find themselves forced into behaviour which goes against their nature and principles. Jenny was able to see from the start of counselling what was happening and why it was uncomfortable for her, but she felt powerless to escape. We talked about what she was afraid of and eventually came to the image of social isolation as a form of annihilation. To lose Jane's approval would be like dying.

After a few sessions in which she explored these two strands, Jenny began to see some connections. In facing the operation, she was genuinely helpless and knew she might die. In facing Jane, she had the option of leaving the group, but was behaving as if she was helpless and might die. She could see that there was a difference: one was real, the other symbolic, but both felt frightening.

From this point she began almost visibly to gain strength. She began to feel as if she had a choice, lots of choices in fact, and we talked about starting with small ones to get in some practice. Jane was in the habit of telling her what to eat, and Jenny had gone along with this to keep the peace, although it often entailed eating things she disliked. She decided to choose one or two things for herself each day in defiance of Jane's dictates. She was very nervous about this, showing the most emotion I had ever witnessed in her, though as usual she fought to control it. The next week she was quietly pleased, reporting that Jane had noticed but ignored her independent decisions.

Progress was far from smooth, and was interrupted by the school holidays when she was due to have her operation. At our last meeting, Jenny admitted being very frightened and finally cried. She was apologetic about showing emotion, and when I reassured her that it was all right to do this with me, she said she couldn't show her family she was afraid because they couldn't bear what was happening to her. When she came back to school having survived the surgery she was able to explore and express her feelings more openly and gained more confidence. She decided not to break with Jane, but found ways to assert herself safely in that relationship, and the feeling of helplessness, both hers and mine, faded perceptibly.

Conclusion

There are several elements in Jenny's story which reappear over and over again in our work here. One is the difficulty with assertiveness, which stems in part from the students' dependence on others for so many of their needs. A certain passivity, not wanting to rock the boat, feeling they should be grateful for help, fearing to upset their already stressed families – all these can affect disabled children and cause them to be unhealthily compliant. Sometimes, they have little sense of their right to inhabit the world at all and need very strong reinforcement of their sense of self-worth.

The counsellors, in their constant struggle to find the best way to help people living with such terrible oppression, must pay steadfast attention to the dual qualities of intimacy and distance. Intimacy, most clearly communicated through empathic connection, congruence and unconditional positive regard is matched with an attitude of distance. This distance not only safeguards the client from the counsellor being overwhelmed and/or swept away in a flood of their own needs, but also finds its source in a faith in the client's own 'capacity . . . to move forward toward maturity' (Rogers 1967). The complex boundary issues that present themselves with this particular client group in this particular setting serve only to highlight the difficult and precarious balance a counsellor needs to strive to maintain. By being both flexible and firm, she may manage both to respond to the reality of these young people's needs without encroaching on their capacity for self-determination and their right to choose. Above all, it is essential that the counsellor values these clients' different abilities and works with the client to celebrate that difference.

Notes

1 Case material is provided by Miranda Ommanney.
2 For a useful and accessible summary of this and other psychodynamic concepts referred or alluded to in this chapter, see Jacobs 1988.

References

Casement, P. (1985) *On Learning From The Patient*, London: Routledge.
Dundas, E. (1978) *Symbols Come Alive in the Sand*, London and Boston, MA: Coventure Ltd.

Earwaker, J. (1992) *Helping and Supporting Students*, Milton Keynes: Open University Press.

Freud, A. (1968) *The Ego and the Mechanisms of Defence*, London: Hogarth Press.

Geldard, K. and Geldard, D. (1999) *Counselling Adolescents*, London: Sage.

Hamilton, C. and Hopegood, L. *Offering Children Confidentiality: Law and Guidance* (A Legal Information Sheet), University of Essex, The Children's Legal Centre: British Association for Counselling.

Jacobs, M. (1988) *Psychodynamic Counselling in Action*, London: Sage.

Lenny, J. (1990) 'Do disabled people need counselling?', in J. Swain, V. Finkelstein, S. French and M. Oliver (eds) *Disabling Barriers, Enabling Environment*, London: Sage and Open University Press.

McGowan, M. (1998) *Guidelines for Good Practice: Counsellors in Schools*, Rugby: British Association for Counselling.

Makin, T. (1995) 'The social model of disability', *Counselling*, 6(4): 274.

Mawson, C. (1994) 'Containing anxiety in work with damaged children', in A. Obholzer and V. Z. Roberts (eds) *The Unconscious at Work*, London: Routledge.

Mearns, D. and Thorne, B. (1988) *Person Centred Counselling In Action*, London: Sage.

Menzies-Lyth, I. (1988) *Containing Anxiety In Institutions*, London: Free Association Books.

Moulster, G. (1998) 'Improving access to counselling for people with learning disabilities', *Learning Disability Practice*, 1(2).

Murgatroyd, S. and Woolfe, R. (1982) 'Parenting and handicap – acceptance of the unacceptable', in *Coping With Crisis – Understanding and Helping People in Need*, London: Harper & Row.

Nelson-Jones, R. (1995) *The Theory and Practice of Counselling Psychology* (2nd edn), London: Cassell.

Reiser, R. and Mason, M. (1990) *Disability Equality in the Classroom: A Human Rights Issue*, London: ILEA.

Rogers, C. R. (1967) *On Becoming A Person*, London: Constable.

Chapter 4

Confidentiality and transference

Philip Hewitt

> Each individual is a component part of numerous groups, he is bound
> by ties of identification in many directions, and he has built up his ego
> ideal upon the most various models. Each individual therefore has a
> share in numerous group minds – those of his race, of his class, of his
> creed, of his nationality, etc.
>
> (Freud 1921: 129)

Theory in context

Confidentiality

When we think of the rule of *confidentiality* in a professional relationship,
it is usually in terms of law and ethical conduct. This focus on codes of
practice both conceals and protects the desire for a 'safe' relationship
through which to explore private feelings and thoughts which occur in
the 'therapeutic alliance'. The prototype of this desire originates in
infantile experience. Object relations theory describes this in terms of the
introjections and identifications of early life: in other words, the complex
interactions which take place between mother and child from the beginning
and from which ultimately we develop a sense of who we are.[1] The loss
of that sense of who we are leads to a wish to return to this time of life,
and it emerges in the growing child and also in the adult as a search for the
lost objects of the infant world (Hinshelwood 1989).

In children and adolescents there is an almost continual process of
recapitulation of earliest experience mingled with the psychological and
biological demands of growing up. In this sense, confidentiality is the
unconscious desire of one person to be held emotionally by another with
the same sense of unconditional care that an infant experiences when held
by its mother. It is problematic when a child or young person who needs

acceptance and love has only a feeling, without words; he or she may experience frustration and inadequacy. Yet the process of confiding is essential. If it invites interest without being seductive or offering false promises, it can enable the client to surmount anxieties of exploitation or of losing control. To whatever degree this is achieved, counselling offers the opportunity to extend the frontiers of personal experience and can lead to growth and change. However, the technicalities of this confiding process are complex, and call for special skills in a counsellor to analyse all the dynamics of the therapeutic relationship, including those arising from its very context.

Confidentiality and context

For significant years in a person's life school has the greatest influence, and may, for some, have greater influence than even the family. Indeed, the state's enforcement of a compulsory school age is no less than a declared intention that this influence should be substantial.

School is an organised imposition of structure and form over individual development, the more so now with the requirement of national standards. It is ironic, then, that psychodynamic counselling offers an opportunity to explore the uniqueness of individuality and personal experience. In a confidential therapeutic relationship with children or adolescents, their subjective feelings of confidence and trust are crucial. Particularly in adolescence, the quest for freedom from parental supervision increases, and at the same time there is a re-working of previous experience, all of which has to interact with school life.

Too much or too little separation becomes a pressure as new milestones are approached. For such reasons, adolescents have deeply personal experiences which often have a quality of immediacy unique to this stage of development. Examples of this are the formation of the closest relationships in both fact and fantasy. Boys and girls are often acutely sensitive about their appearances while lacking insight into their wishes for acceptability and inner contentment. Rather, the experience is concrete and without dispute, so that at this time a preoccupation with what is normal or abnormal is often a dominant feature of adolescents' lives.

Disillusionment and mistrust of adult authority prompts adolescent acting out, usually physical in nature, as an attempt to break physical and psychological dependencies and deal with intolerable internal pressures. Preoccupations with body and explorations of bodily capacities are also a dominant feature of adolescence. Sexual drives enable adolescents to sustain a momentum and sequester a sense of intimacy with 'the self' which is explored both in relation to peers and in newly acquired opportunities for solitude. Any one or more of these aspects of adolescent experience may be brought to the counselling relationship. This presents the counsellor with a formidable task of integration which stretches thinking capacity as he or she is flooded with a *mélange* of stimuli which detail the session.

Transference

In psychoanalytic theory, transference is the phenomenon through which a patient projects feelings and ideas from past relationships on to the therapist and relates to the therapist as if he were one of those people. The transference in its broadest sense is the sum of all the feelings towards the therapist. It is unconscious but becomes available clinically through the words, associations, dreams, parapraxes (slips of the tongue) and feelings of the client.

The concept of transference was first developed by Freud from his clinical work, where he realised that the interpretation of dreams and parapraxes also yielded important information about unconscious life. At first he saw transference as an obstacle to understanding which had to be analysed out of the analyst's mind. Since Freud, Klein (1946), Winnicott (1947), Heimann (1950) and others have all added substantially to the theory of transference and countertransference – the latter being the thoughts and feelings the therapist may have towards his client (see also Chapter 5) – such that it is today the cornerstone of therapeutic work.

Transference and the clinical context

All clinicians will be familiar with the experience of being overwhelmed with material from the client. Only with the benefit of some distance from the session, and often in supervision, do things become clearer. For these reasons an understanding of transference is indispensable to the clinician. My own classical psychoanalytic training was based upon this concept.

Years ago, when I first started working with students and school-age clients, I had to re-examine how my knowledge of the transference might be used. This was especially so in the light of all that I have said so far about the context of school life and how, unlike a psychoanalytic session, a school counselling session is very much located in the present concerns of educational progress, position at school and, often, statutory requirements.

The case example which follows illustrates how I found myself thinking about the transference both in terms of therapeutic process and, within that, the clamouring of young people to be understood. The explicit context of school is one in which children are expected to conform, either in a culture of positive encouragement or sometimes through coercive measures. In addition to this, the complexity of a child's transference to the school counsellor will be assembled according to previous experience such as the primary models which are available in parents and teachers, and the way in which he or she is managing developmental changes. On this occasion I was asked to see John by his tutor, who told me briefly that John had problems at home and that his work in school was deteriorating.

Clinical work

John

My consulting room door opened, and I saw a cheerful, friendly, fifteen-year-old boy. For a first meeting I felt that he entered my room with an unusual and disarming air of confidence. Over the next few weeks, I became increasingly aware of the contrast between John's outward appearance and the feelings of personal inadequacy being suggested by the appalling story of his family breakdown. This was characterised by the father's drug addiction, which had led to an acrimonious divorce years before, as a result of which the mother was still full of hatred towards him. John's story of failure was almost unbearable, and through my own feelings, in other words, my countertransference, I became aware of a growing need to reassure him. This was particularly strong as it seemed that, on the one hand, here was a young client with such promise, but on the other, such damage to overcome.

It also struck me that the circumstances in which John had been referred were rather vague. The teacher had not been able to be specific about what the problem was and had expressed only a general feeling that John needed help. Only gradually did it become apparent that this was a reflection, both of his difficulty, and of the school's inability, to recognise the pain of a boy who presented so cheerfully and hopefully while carrying with him a sense of being ruined inside. Now that John was at last being understood, there seemed to be a reversal of positions. The school, through me, was beginning to understand, and John was confused. The question was whether John would allow me to work with him on the basis of acknowledging how he felt inside, or whether we had to go along with the denial which had sustained him so far. John found his own way of resolving this question.

After a few months, and following the summer vacation, he started to miss appointments. Once more I found myself wondering about my own feelings of failure and the wish to go into the school and look for John. This would have been breaking boundaries and confidentiality. Even if John had given me consent to do so, I knew that we had been working on things which were implicit – to do with his internal world – things which were part of an emotional exchange between us. I could not add value to anything which might occur in a counselling session by trying to be something other than his counsellor outside the session. The fact that I could not do this, namely break boundaries and confidentiality, put me even more in touch with feelings of inadequacy, especially with regard to John's needs for a firm and consistent parental interest to be taken in him.

In my countertransference I discovered feelings which I believe related to early maternal deprivation, so that at times I had to confront my preoccupation with trying to 'save' John from himself. What I came to realise was that he was entrusting to me a gamut of developmental experience, including the immediacy of his relationships at school. There were no answers to his problems as such, but my task was to keep on trying to resolve the difficulties within the only structures available, those of school and the therapeutic milieu of counselling. My effort was to support this, and to allow the transferential desire contained in the notion of confidentiality to develop. This required working in the countertransference, with the pressures in the countertransference of being more than a counsellor, and providing just *elements* of the unconditional love which he so desperately sought. In short, I experienced a wish to provide the substance in John's life which was missing – to be the 'good parent'.

I considered that the wish to be the 'good parent' was a familiar response to the unbearable pain of insufficiency with which John was himself struggling. At the same time I had to wonder about John's façade of optimism, and how this could be such a beguiling device to conceal the confused feelings with which he needed help. It seemed to me that as I got closer to this sense of truth about his reason for consulting me, John stopped coming to the sessions completely. As I had got to know John quite well by now, I felt the loss of not seeing him, save for sightings around the school. This experience once again made me think of the attenuated relationship which John must have had with his father. In other words, there were times when there was no real contact with his father, and John himself was left wondering what was happening.

A year or so later John reappeared, this time looking more physically mature but less determinedly optimistic. I saw this as evidence of some progress in that he may have internalised something from our first contact. In fact, he was now concerned about his relationships with girls. Among his peers he had achieved a reputation as being a 'bit of a lad', but at the same time I remembered how he had conveyed a sense of false optimism and internal desolation when he first appeared. Now, with more of a sense of maturity, he was concerned about his reputation as he began to talk about the increasing difference between the way he really felt and the way he thought he was seen by others. I saw this not only as his way of telling me that he recognised that it was something of a front, but also that it was very difficult to change.

From a growing confidence of feeling that I might be on the right track with John, I could think more in terms of my own countertransference. I imagined that John's peers were easily caught up in similar feelings about him – feelings of inadequacy which led them to avoid making real contact with him. It was relatively easy for their behaviour, and his, to become subsumed in normative, adolescent, sexualised acting out. Now I began to feel I understood why John had returned to see me. Being more senior in the school, he was faced with what must have felt to him an impossible task: that of connecting the apparent idolisation from the girls he went with to the pain of his growing consciousness of the loss of a meaningful relationship with his father.

Although John now talked eagerly, sometimes pouring out his feelings, I was confronted by an even greater sense of futility as his final term at school drew to a close. When I learned that John had failed to obtain the necessary grades for a place at university, I realised just how much my client had not coped with the task of integrating his emotional and intellectual life at the end of his school career. With hindsight, I saw myself as having been trapped in a rolling process which reflected John's own predicament of denying his internal deprivation. My task had unfolded as one of holding the transference, both to me as an individual, and also to that part of me which John experienced as a responsive part of the school. Once again I was prompted by the need to keep in mind my own context as school counsellor. The clinical context was as a part of the school timetable and not a psychoanalytic practice. Therefore, in my countertransference, I had to think about the complexity of the part which I played as a member of the school in the re-enactment of environmental failure which John may have unconsciously courted. My task in the confidential counselling relationship was to try and help John to understand that danger, and to support him, in the short term, in dealing with the numerous difficulties which had already accumulated in his young life.

During our sessions, which stretched over nearly three years, John made many disclosures of a deeply personal nature. Some of what he told me, particularly revelations about difficulties with teachers who were pushed up to and sometimes over the limits of professional conduct by him, clearly infringed school rules. In this regard, there were two main processes at work. Firstly, I was always working with the boundaries of confidentiality in my countertransference as part of a dynamic process of John's transference. The pressure which I experienced to look for John when he did not come to sessions is an example of the intensity of my own transference to him. Yet, as I have discussed above, it would have been disastrous for me to do so. Then there was the wish to intervene when, according to John, teachers had acted unprofessionally. I identified with him to the extent of thinking, 'If *my* son had told me his teacher had spoken to him abusively like this, I would want to take the matter further.'

Secondly, John was trying to sort out internal and external realities as part of his chaotic developmental process. This struggle revealed itself in the fluctuations of trust, confidence, and relatedness to the counsellor (as part of his relationship to the school), unfolding in a pattern of intense contact, then none for months, until the last few months before leaving school for good. (And of course I had to work through my own counter-transference feelings of confusion, worry and inadequacy throughout this intense time.) My angry feelings about appointments which were not kept and sessions being used to rubbish everything about school could not easily be interpreted to John in a meaningful way. However, it was crucial that I held the extremes of his feelings through my own sense of the unconscious desire to be the good parent, part of which is tolerating the child's rage which previously had been suppressed or not understood. This psychodynamic way of thinking enabled John to go on thinking for himself about aspects of his life, so that he could take more personal responsibility for his own feelings. My understanding of the transference helped me to see that confidentiality provides an opportunity for the client to experience the counsellor and school as a containing relationship. It seems to me that the greater the deprivation, the greater is the need for the child to be able to experience school in this way. Thus the rules and law which govern confidentiality provide a framework for a potentially quite profound emotional experience.

Context revisited

Transference and the school context

In John's life it appeared that school was second only in influence to his family of origin, but in this regard he is not exceptional. At best, parents, teachers and the children and young people themselves are drawn into a collaboration to make this possible. At worst, schools and parents rival each other for authority over the child. Throughout the school years this relationship is played out. One example might be the assertion that children must not miss time at school for the sake of holidays with parents, and the parents' challenge to this principle. Clichés that school knows best and expectations that education should be able to solve all social evils are often countered by disparagement of academic standards and accusations of school life being irrelevant.

The child–parent–school triangle is a dynamic relationship fuelled by various aspirations, frustrations and the wish to prepare for and obtain advantage in life. Indeed, school life itself can be an experience organised by a range of feelings which include shame, guilt, competition, ambition and fears of inadequacy. For such reasons, a school goes to considerable lengths to counteract negative effects by instituting rules, policies, staff training and communication with parents in order to ensure that the school environment is a safe place in which to live and learn. Children and staff are encouraged to identify with their school and work towards common aims – this may be referred to variously as 'school spirit', 'team work' or 'our community'. Alumni organisations extend this idea and are the result of an explicit intention to foster an enduring relationship. In addition, parental expectations of a school often find their source in a desire to compensate for deficiencies in home life or the search for social improvement. Thus a school is the object of considerable projection and a target for transferred feelings.

Children have to manage this three-cornered relationship, which is made the more difficult where there is limited consensus between the parties. In this relationship an Oedipal stage (see Chapter 1) is set which presents many opportunities for splitting – a process by which one party is seen as *all* bad and another as *all* good – and pairing as each party attempts to obtain supremacy in relation to the other. The school counsellor occupies a special position in relation to working through the triangular relationship, often having to hold a balance between an unresponsive institution, the desperation experienced by the child as a result of unmet needs and the 'depressive' realisation by the parents that their own wishes for compensation through their child's education cannot be satisfied.

This was illustrated by another case in which Peter, a very successful student, threatened to sabotage his career at school by dabbling with drugs. The parents, who were separated, redoubled their squabbling when Peter got into trouble at school. Although he was doing well academically, his parents entered into mutual recriminations about the choice of school. Peter's mother blamed the school for everything that had gone wrong because she had wanted him educated in America, where 'everything was better', while the father said that it was her attitude which was the problem. It was as though they completely denied their own responsibility by landing it on the other. In terms of a culture of experimentation with drugs, Peter's behaviour could be seen, to some extent, as normative peer group activity. However, he was also angry with both parents, whom he was trying to please, and being torn apart in the process of trying to re-route the hatred between them.

Another aspect of the transference is the part that the media play in shaping or confirming versions of behaviour and various roles which human beings take. This is a significant source of information as to how a child understands a meeting with the counsellor. In most of these familiar constructions there is a basic assumption that the older person has authority over the younger. In fact, the relationship between young and old is usually characterised by a battle about freedom and responsibility. The counsellor must have an understanding of this tension as an essential step towards building confidence and demonstrating that close attention is being paid to the way the client feels. It is precisely in this aspect of building a therapeutic alliance where confidentiality begins. Part of the difficulty is that important signals about the emotional state of the client flow through the transference simultaneously, revealing how the conscious and unconscious desire for confidentiality is intertwined with the transference itself.

John was also representative of the many clients who start counselling with the sense that the catastrophe has already happened. The early stages of my work with him often suggested that he was assessing whether I was trustworthy. Contrasted with this sensitive process, most young clients are inclined to make peremptory judgements about complicated matters such as a counselling session. When asked to put into words what they feel, they respond minimally with 'Don't know', 'Fine', or 'It was crap', expressing dislike or denial of interest and guarding their sense of independence.

The institutional transference

The transference includes the child's *actual* relationship with the school and the counsellor as they move through different cycles of the year. In this way, working through personal experience as well as the qualitative experience in clinical work is part of a skill which the psychodynamic counsellor uses, and it is central to an understanding of the therapeutic relationship. However controversial the distinction of interchanging subjective feelings with objective feelings may be, this dynamic interchange gives a richness to what the psychodynamic counsellor postulates as *clinical* experience. It is both a disposition in the clinician and a training which allows this, with some caution as to how it is applied, to be a viable and at times an essential way of processing and understanding material (Holmes and Perrin 1997). This also means that the school counsellor can think about his or her relationship to the school in terms of the transference and what he or she represents at any one time to the institution. Sometimes there is even direct evidence of the transference to him or her.

So, soon after my appointment as school counsellor, I was alarmed one day when told that the students doubted my capacity to be confidential. No explanation was given until later, when there was the opportunity to discuss the charge with some of the students. It turned out to be true, that the perception of some students was that I was untrustworthy, but no one could actually substantiate the accusation. Eventually, a student volunteered the information that others thought I 'looked treacherous'. This remarkable disclosure alerted me to a very different state of affairs, namely that I was the subject of a negative and potentially destructive transference.

I knew from other clinical experience that there was anxiety about acknowledging feelings in the school and that maintaining a façade of confidence was the priority. I had never seen myself as 'looking treacherous', let alone 'being treacherous'. I knew that this was not right, but also, in a backhanded way, it was a compliment about how the power of the counsellor was being seen. However, it suggested an extremely high level of anxiety in the school, namely that the students were being faced with a choice about confiding issues which previously might be avoided. Therefore it seemed that my new post was having a dynamic impact on the whole institution by altering the shape, i.e. introducing a fourth point to the child–parent–school relationship.

The accusation about my lack of confidentiality reinforced the idea even more of the unconscious desire for a special relationship, which in a sense was perceived as a poisoned chalice, filled with treachery. This was confirmed when further criticism was received that I used the school crest on writing paper, suggesting that I was not independent. Over the next few weeks I had to establish myself through talking to groups of students, and on one occasion by addressing the whole school about my position and specifically about confidentiality. I could not be sure what the students heard me say but, almost as an act of faith, my intention was at the very least not to obstruct the possibility of a different transference. I know now that, at least for some, this has happened.

For others, my position feeds their ambivalence about dependency on the school, and they usually prefer to keep their distance from me and other adults. For this reason, and those described above, the role is difficult and often isolated. Part of the institutional transference is that the counsellor is often identified with failure, dealing with the casualties of life. Where there is responsive leadership in a school, the counsellor will feel the benefit of the headteacher's ability to accept criticism and work with omnipresent schismatic forces within the school. There is a world of difference between a headteacher who can hold the tensions of uncertainty in dealing with complex problems and responsibilities, as opposed to one who splits the complexity into simple decrees over right and wrong to defend himself against the anxiety of the difficulties inherent in school life. When a counsellor has the support of the senior teachers, it implies that there is a shared understanding of their respective roles. Where that support is missing, it is likely to mean that the counsellor is no more than tolerated. In the case of John, rather like the client himself, I had felt exposed and alone with the responsibility. When I shared this feeling with a colleague, she wisely pointed out that this was most likely part of John's own experience which was left with me.

In another case I received enormous support from a girl's housemaster. Ann was not a popular girl in school. She tended to be a loner and had a rather surly disposition. When her father died suddenly, her negative attitudes seemed to increase, effectively driving off support which she might otherwise have received from peers and teachers. Ann elected to seek counselling, and began to confide how unhappy she was, and that she had, in fact, had a very poor relationship with her father. Aware of her position with people at school, she asked me to speak to her housemaster, whom she respected but thought would not understand. Although I knew this would change the nature of our therapeutic relationship and the way she saw how I might help, it seemed necessary to play an active part in helping her to make this link. There were many difficulties, including some truancy, but eventually the willingness of the housemaster to understand, and his capacity to care for a very unhappy teenager, worked as a positive influence in her life at school. Thus my action seemed to pay off, and the important ingredient here was that we were able to cooperate. In spite of her attitude, Ann actually wanted to make things work at school, although she did not want the housemaster to know too much about the difficulties of her home life. The housemaster, as if representing school pastoral care, was himself able to detect this in her and respect my boundaries of confidentiality.

Conclusions

Confidentiality is the experience of being in a relationship where there is an unconditional interest from an adult who does not off-load his problems or value judgements. It refers to the sense of being with an adult who has come to terms with his or her own needs and does not use the counselling relationship as a concrete expression of unmet frustration. At the same time, the counsellor, still within a professional framework, has to be available to the feelings of the client, whatever they may be; otherwise, psychodynamic counselling will atrophy. In practice, to achieve the result suggested here is very difficult, for the counsellor is but a 'component part' of the wider context, which includes his or her own life as well as the triangular relationship with the school. As 'a component part of numerous groups' (Freud 1921) he or she has to engage with the dynamics of the wider group and prevailing mores if only at the level of dynamic conceptualisation.

Robert May (1988) describes his experience in terms of being a 'voice' among a number in the institution: a 'voice' rather than a 'role' because he wants to make clear the importance of 'being' as opposed to 'behaving', the latter usually being associated with a discussion of roles. The immediate relevance of this is to underline the desire in the counsellor to apply his skills as truly as possible (in the sense of being). At the same time it is important to acknowledge the contradiction that 'technique' strays towards 'behaving' rather than 'being'. This appeared many times in my countertransference in a disguised form, as my wish to respond spontaneously to the demands of the young client seeking a reparative relationship with a parental figure. Analysing this feeling makes me suspicious of collusion with the client and of 'playing at' being the good parent. This whole struggle can be likened to the adolescent developmental struggle of coping with feelings rather than gratifying spontaneous urges. In the Robert May sense, and essential to understanding the transference in order to promote good emotional health, an individual also has to strive towards 'being' as well as 'acting'. This is as important for psychodynamic counselling work as it is intrinsic to the social and psychological development of children.

Through transference, the counsellor receives important information about a client's emotional state. This is discrete knowledge in the sense that it is not tangible and can only be represented through a description of the relationship. When John entered my consulting room, a process began in which he conveyed aspects of his experience for which he could find no other outlet at the time. The client was able to break down his sense of isolation and begin to allow himself to know things which previously had been too painful to know. During this process there was a small shift towards facing his feelings of failure and towards 'being' rather than behaving destructively. In the transference I experienced the feelings of inadequacy and the unmet dependency needs of the client, which became more acute as his time at school drew to a close. There was no way in which a school could compensate for deficiencies in John's life. However, it was able to provide a structure, as well as an education, through which these deficiencies could emerge so that he could begin to work on them for himself. Essential to this emergence is the understanding held in a school (again like the hidden desire in confidentiality) that this process is part of the task, and therefore there is no place for retaliatory responses to children in its care.

Confidentiality creates a membrane around the clinical relationship which has a human endeavour at its core. The transference to the confidentiality of the counsellor might be as a capacious parent or a seductive and manipulative one. The sense of what is going on is often slightly out of reach of our words and can only be felt. Armed with this knowledge, our techniques, and a willingness to work through and be honest with ourselves about our feelings, a door can be opened wider for the client. This must be understood in order to do justice to what is an actual experience within the transference and not just a theoretical abstraction or something put in place for legal requirements. It is possible to communicate and receive communications, sometimes slightly out of reach of words, but in a way which permits the senses to play with each other towards both knowing and feeling; knowing through our feelings. It is the expression and enactment of an early desire to hold and be held. This can be understood gradually, through the transference, as the counsellor takes in more and more about his client.

In addition, the counsellor has to be aware of the wider context of school and home, where clients sometimes consent to the exchange of information. I do not believe informed consent to disclosure about the discrete aspects of the transference, or the sense of 'being' experienced in the relationship, is easy to give, or for that matter should be sought. My work with John exemplifies an experience of confidentiality through transferential material. John and the other clients have been disguised such that the real person could not recognise himself from the facts. Nevertheless, I hope that if anyone who has ever had the experience of being a client were to read this book, he or she might recognise something about the meaning of their experience with a counsellor which is entirely personal to him or her. Equally, I hope this might be true for anyone working with young people, that they too might share in the sense of confidentiality which I have tried to describe.

Note

1 For a fuller account of object relations theory and some of the processes mentioned here, see Chapter 11.

References

Freud, S. (1921) 'A differentiating grade in the ego in group psychology', in *The Standard Edition* of the *Complete Psychological Works of Sigmund Freud Vol. XVIII*, ed. J. Strachey, London: Hogarth.

Heimann, P. (1950) 'On countertransference', *The International Journal of Psycho-Analysis*, 31: 81–84.

Hinshelwood, R. D. (1989) *A Dictionary of Kleinian Thought*, London: Free Association Books.

Holmes, G. and Perrin, A. (1997) 'Countertransference: What is it? What do we do with it?', *Psychodynamic Counselling*, 3(3): 263–277.

Klein, M. (1946) 'Notes on some schizoid mechanisms', in *Envy and Gratitude and Other Works 1946–1963*, London: Hogarth, 1975.

May, R. (1988) 'Boundaries and voices in college psychotherapy', in *Psychoanalytic Psychotherapy in a College Context*, New York: Praeger.

Winnicott, D. W. (1947) 'Hate in the countertransference', in *Through Paediatrics to Psycho-analysis*, London: Hogarth, 1982.

Chapter 5

Is it safe enough to learn?

Ferelyth Watt

> One starts somewhere – where the learner *is*. And one starts *whenever* the student arrives to begin his *career as a learner*.
>
> (Bruner 1960)

Introduction

In this chapter I share some of my experience as a psychodynamically trained counsellor working as a peripatetic special needs teacher in mainstream schools. I present and explore some of my thoughts in relation to an insistent theme which I have come to think of as: Is it safe enough to learn? Here, safety is concerned primarily with the conditions required for a child to feel secure enough to engage in the learning process.

Children who are referred to learning support services for learning, behavioural or emotional problems are often those who are communicating deep anxieties about the interplay between internal, unconscious elements rooted in early relationships, and the external aspects of the learning and social environment of the school. In turn, these may reflect the child's experience of difficulties outside the school, particularly at home.

Children most clearly raising the question of safety in the learning process are those 20 per cent identified as being in special educational need (DES 1978). These children are considered to have 'significantly greater difficulty in learning than the majority of children of the same age' or 'have a disability which either prevents or hinders [them] from making use of educational facilities of the kind generally available in school' (DES 1988).

It is also reported that in any class group, at any time, 16 per cent of pupils may find themselves in need of specialist support (ACE 1989). Indeed, I believe these children articulate the anxieties of many children. For learning is a complex and difficult task demanding change, and requiring the learner – of any age – to risk the stability and certainty of the status quo for the relative uncertainty associated with different perceptions borne of new knowledge, skills or understanding.

In my view, the need to acknowledge and understand children's communications is crucial in providing a school environment that is safe enough in which to learn. The particular contribution made by professionals working from a psychodynamic perspective is in trying to understand the part played by emotional life and the unconscious aspects involved in the learning process.

As a cross-phase (three to sixteen years) area support teacher, I not only work with pupils (groups and individuals) but also with teachers, professionals, parents/carers and managers, applying psychodynamic concepts to assist them in thinking about the children in a way that is responsive rather than reactive and which better enables them in their task of providing a facilitative learning environment. In this chapter, however, I focus, in the main, on my work with individual pupils. Drawing on two case examples, I show how my understanding of infantile and child development, informed by psychoanalytic theory and developmental psychology, is applied in an educational setting to help children reach the point where they feel safe enough to learn.[1]

Theory

Central to my understanding of safety is Winnicott's (1960) concept of 'holding' (see Chapter 2). So too is Bion's (1962) view of the receptive mother as a 'container' for her baby's 'projections' of raw experience – those incomprehensible anxiety-ridden states resulting from the impact of such things as hunger, a fever or a sudden loud noise (see chapters 1 and 11). In a sense, without even knowing it, the 'good-enough mother' (Winnicott 1960) uses the feelings or body-states, aroused in her by her anxious baby's inarticulate communications, to help her understand her baby's state of mind. It is this understanding that allows her to respond to his needs appropriately. In time, and with many repetitions, the baby's experience of this process – of a mother who tolerates, makes sense of and aptly responds to his anxieties – promotes in him an increasing trust in the containability of all types of experience and a growing confidence in his own capacity to tolerate, make sense of and learn from them. In short, he acquires the capacity to think.

The mediating process which the good-enough mother engages in has its parallel in the process of counselling. The anxious child may, unwittingly, use the counsellor by projecting into her the raw uncontained experience about which he finds it difficult to think. The feelings that this arouses in the counsellor are referred to as countertransference, and the counsellor needs to use her countertransference feelings to further her understanding of the child's anxieties, difficulties, wishes and so on. These concepts – holding, projection, containment, countertransference – help to explain the methodology of a psychodynamic counsellor working with children.

Theory in context

The service, the referral and the school

I work in a team context – one of three teams, each servicing a separate group of schools within the borough. Each team is generalist, comprising teachers with specific training, skills and experience in various areas of special educational need, for example: reading recovery; behavioural skills; counselling; visual or other sensory impairment. My own area of expertise is with children and young people, singly or in groups, who are troubling to teachers because their behaviour is difficult to manage or unusual in the context of their peers: those who are not learning or those who relate to teachers and other pupils in ways that evoke feelings which are unmanageable or especially troublesome. My role is to provide a support service not only for the children themselves but for their parents, teachers and support staff, for other liaising professionals and at an organisational level, for heads, managers and staff teams.

The manner in which pupils are referred to the team and thus to myself is reviewed, revised and updated almost constantly. This is indicative of the uncertainty surrounding the long-term existence of the service. Rather than elaborate the detail of the referral process, I shall indicate it in diagrammatic form (Figure 1).

In my view, it is essential that adequate time be allocated to gathering information, assessing the situation and the nature of the problem before making any plans to work directly with the referral. This information-gathering process includes discussing the referral with the referrer. Frequently, staff feel beleaguered by the multiplicity of demands made upon them and call for help when a situation has reached a crisis or become chronic and unbearable. The decision to discuss and meet about a referral is often met with anger and resentment, as any delay in relieving the worry is seen as prevarication, even persecution. A fine balance has to be drawn, so that the tension between the need to act and the need to give time for thinking about issues raised by the referrer and one's own role can be

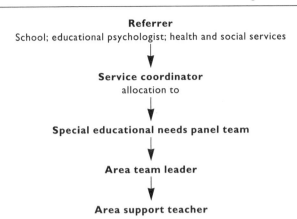

Figure 1 Education support service referral process

experienced as a positive contribution, likely to assist the intervention rather than be damaging to it.

One reason for the importance of the information-gathering process is that the referred problem may well be symptomatic of conflict somewhere in the system, involving: the child and their experience of learning; the family group and their attitude towards 'the problem', the school and learning; and the teaching and non-teaching staff's own unconscious contributions to the teaching and learning processes (Salzberger-Wittenberg *et al.* 1983) and the wider school system.

At times, the work is directly with the referred child, either in the classroom or on a withdrawal basis or even a mixture of both. At others, it is more appropriate to work with a whole class or group. This is particularly so when the referral of an individual seems, on consideration, to be articulating concerns of other children in class.

> A secondary school student was referred for her unexpected under-achievement, notably in English. Work with her revealed anxiety about the impending competition required as exams loomed. In addition, however, working with the teacher in class revealed widespread underlying concerns among students about being competitive with each other in some aspects of the curriculum, whilst being required to work collaboratively in others.

Sometimes it is more appropriate to work with a teacher, member of the support staff or parent/carer, facilitating their thinking about how best to help the child manage his difficulties. Indeed, there are occasions when, while discussing a child, it becomes evident that the teacher is acting out of character and is puzzled by this. Once a trusting enough relationship has developed, it can be useful to discuss with the teacher the reasons for this uncharacteristic behaviour. If teachers are able to see how it is possible to use their own feelings and behaviours to help understand a child, they may be better able to offer a containing experience for the child, as well as gaining some emotional relief themselves.

> Ms S expressed her concern and irritation about J's constant clinging manner and fawning attempts to gain attention. As she explored her concern, it became evident that she was also worried by the way she felt goaded to act in a harsh and uncompromising way. On further reflection arising from our discussions, she realised that this echoed her own uncompromising attitude to her own wish to be liked by others. Understanding her part in the dynamic relationship with J helped Ms S to think differently about the girl and enabled her to be more accommodating. In turn, the child's behaviour became less clinging.

The frequency and duration of any intervention depends upon the nature of the problem and the approach being made to change it. Working in a preventive, contextually-aware fashion, which is able to utilise multi-disciplinary assessments, classroom observations, supervision groups for teaching and support staff, as well as liaison with parents/carers, can contribute enormously to the task of developing and maintaining an environment in which it is safe enough to learn. It is regrettable, therefore, that increasing competition for learning support resources has resulted in staff being drawn away from such work with children not yet having a Statement of Educational Need.[2] Most crucially, it is regrettable that there is little or no time safeguarded, on a regular basis, for thinking about issues.

Clinical work

> The attitude towards the acquisition and recognition of new knowledge is an expression of the relationship to all knowledge, old and new: if knowledge-objects are internalised ambivalently, they will tyrannise bearers.
>
> (Figlio 1991: 90)

I continue by offering two case examples, selected because they demonstrate how helpful it can be to try and understand a child's communications as indications of the child's internal world and how he interacts with the school environment. In each case, the clinical work includes further information gathering through observing each child in his educational context before working directly with him in a counselling capacity. While it is highly desirable to work in a room designated for counselling, and at regular times, this is often difficult to manage and it may be essential for the counsellor to deal with this at an organisational level from the outset. However, the counselling is not necessarily confined to the consultation room but may take place within the classroom context if it is seen to be beneficial.

Robert: rubbers in the glue pot

Thinking about Robert in context

Robert, aged ten, was liked by his teachers, most of whom, finding him endearing, adopted a maternal attitude towards him. Nevertheless, he was referred by his class teacher and head because of concern about his considerable underachievement, his limited social skills, his lack of friendships, his lying, stealing (he was also well known to local police for shoplifting) and hoarding, as well as his unkempt appearance. In addition, there were long-standing concerns about the care that he and his three siblings received in the maternal home, following the tragic death of the father four years previously.

Robert found learning full of unpleasant uncertainties and difficulties. He had little conception of the excitement and sense of mastery that can be a part of the learning process. Initially, I decided to observe Robert in his class group for a few hours, from registration to first break. As a visitor to the class, I was introduced as someone who was interested in what happens in schools.

Robert shuffled into the room, nearly ten minutes late as usual. He looked waif-like, thin, his black skin almost grey with dryness. His clothes were dirty and too large for him. He then began moving around the room in an agile way, as though having a light physical presence. He seemed to slip and slide between both people and furniture. From time to time he made a comment to another child – one made in passing – and was rarely in the vicinity long enough to receive a reply. It was as though Robert's relationships were devoid of lasting contact.

Robert approached English and maths tasks circuitously: his pencil needed sharpening, the sharpener could not be found; he needed a rubber, which one should he choose?; he needed a ruler to underline the exercise and date, but of course didn't have one; he barely managed to begin before it was break time.

Like many children in distress, Robert quickly made eye contact, then studiously avoided me. Watching him evoked a host of feelings: maternal concern and caring, curiosity about him and his family life, as well as a sense of desperation. I was also aware of something about his manner which gave the impression that he might challenge me. From experience, I understood this as evidence of his wish to be contained, and that such a challenge was likely to feature infantile phantasies (see Chapter 11) of omnipotence – those phantasies that give expression to the belief that feelings or wishes can in themselves change the external world, and are characterised by fears about aggressive and envious feelings being totally destructive and unmanageable (Klein 1921).

I watched Robert with curiosity as he began a language task. He delayed the start by getting out his tray, rummaging through sheets of crumpled paper, pencils, cars, rubber bands, pieces of blue tack and so on. Finally, he picked out some rubbers – nearly two handfuls – and carefully dropped each one into a glue pot. He did all this as if completely oblivious to his surroundings – in particular, his teacher and her likely irritation. Once finished, he resumed his efforts to start writing.

Subsequently, I learned that Robert had done this sort of thing before. His teacher considered such behaviour rather bizarre but agreed that it seemed to be a communication that might, in time, be understood sufficiently to put into words. I saw my task as trying to understand Robert's actions and to work with him to find words which might give expression to some of the feelings that underlay his behaviour.

Thinking with Robert

I worked with Robert twice weekly for a total of four-and-a-half hours, for a period of two years. Our sessions took place both in class and outside in a large comfortable room that housed the library and numerous work stations. Our beginnings were extremely difficult. Initially, Robert behaved like a child younger than his age. Wanting sweets during the session, he would always have a handy supply. He sat with nose running, shoes undone and trousers slipping down over slim hips. When I tried to manage the limits of our sessions in the form of keeping his sweets until playtime, he frequently responded by dashing off to the cloakroom, ostensibly to go to the loo but often returning with a toy or torn computer game magazine. Similarly, my comments or interpretations about his behaviour gave rise to characteristic defences such as denying that he might be worried about being with a strange person. Despite these defensive responses, however, I think he was also aware that he needed me to be prepared to sit alongside him, while he worked very hard to defy me and tried to render me useless. In short, he needed to test my capacity to stay with him, to think, to bear him and his hate.

To some extent, all children test an adult in this kind of way, checking to see that he or she can provide adequate containment so that they can get on and play or learn as they need to do. Some children, however, need to test the adults who care and work with them many times, and often with such intensity that it does feel almost unbearable. Children, like Robert, come to school needing a 'stable emotional situation in which they can exercise their emotional lability, a group of which they can gradually become a part; a group that can be tested out as to its ability to withstand aggression and to tolerate aggressive ideas' (Winnicott 1946). It was very important, therefore, for me to maintain my capacity to think and manage the boundaries of the relationship without retaliation and to continue to work on the basis that Robert was searching for a secure base (Bowlby 1978; and see Chapter 6); a place from which he could begin to make exploratory moves without feeling so empty that he needed to shore up his store of internal resources *en route* with sweets and toys.

For several months I felt utterly hopeless and unable to see any signs of progress. I also believed that I was being persecutory and depriving by trying to keep limits and not acceding to his wishes for immediate gratification. My understanding of these feelings as manifestations of my countertransference helped me to better understand Robert's state of mind and to continue my approach despite his opposition.

Gradually, our relationship began to change. Robert became able to engage with me in a range of learning tasks and to do so for increasing periods before having to give up and resort to the comfort of sitting, sweets in hand, close by me. After about seven months, at the end of one of our sessions, Robert turned to me with a smile saying, 'See you next week'. I felt delighted. Wonderful! Until then, despite Robert's interest in telling the time, he had no sense of it, had been ignorant of the structure of his school week and of any continuity to our sessions.

Following this event, I was able to encourage Robert to try more things: to choose books he liked the look of, to tell stories that I would scribe, to use the computer for writing, to learn to tell the time. Towards the end of our first year, I introduced Robert to a book called *The Magic Mirror*, which described and illustrated the journey of a boy who goes through a magic mirror to find a surreal world before stepping back through the mirror into the real world. After reading it together, Robert made his own story. He said he 'saw some strange things'. These included topsy-turvy images of mother figures in the sky, dogs taking men for walks and wild animals being kept at bay by heroic boys with flutes. Towards the end, Robert's character 'saw a blue river and he jumped in the river and he swam backwards and then a shark came along and then he killed it'.

This story was produced over a period of five weeks. During this time, Robert demonstrated feelings of anger and rage. In the course of this journey, under the guise of his story's characters, he was able to find words and give meaning to some of the unexpressed rage and fear he felt about the experience of having been parted from his mother at the age of three, and then, on being reunited with her, of finding her pregnant with another child. Any rivalrous feelings he had felt towards his father or his yet-to-be-born brother had been overshadowed by the unexpected death of his father shortly afterwards. Thus actual experience had become fused with his own phantasies about ruthlessness – about Oedipal anxieties (see Chapter 1) – including his fear that his omnipotent wishes had killed his father – and about sibling rivalry. Robert's attacks on what I had to offer were an exploration of the possibility of expressing these feelings – to see if they could be managed without resulting in disaster. My understanding of the symbolism of the rubbers and glue was that they were a manifestation of Robert's wish for cohesion and integration, as well as his anxiety about his aggressive wishes arising, for example, from rivalrous feelings. Unable to manage these charged and complex emotions on his own, Robert could only respond in an infantile, concrete way, by using actual things as if they were his otherwise unmanageable feelings. Robert had sought a way of trying to manage externally his deeply troubling psychological problem, and the rubbers in the glue pot represented a compromise solution to his dilemma. Yet, it was clear that Robert had hope, and his own perseverance with our task touched me deeply.

Our work together ended before either of us would have liked. More could have been done but Robert *had* changed. He said that he felt he 'walked taller' than he had done when we first met. At the end of our work together, Robert's relationships with his peers, in and out of school, had improved. He seemed to be able to take risks as a learner and to approach tasks with an attitude of greater self-confidence. Evidence of this lay in his improved reading and writing. He could tolerate criticism, making mistakes and not knowing things. He could also bear to show his dependency and to ask for help from adults when required. He expressed and coped with all kinds of feelings, most noticeably anger, sadness, curiosity, excitement and joy.

John: holding with a gaze

Thinking about John in context

John, aged eight, was referred because of his class teacher's concern about the uneven state of his cognitive and emotional development. For example, his reading age was five years above his actual age, yet his comprehension of certain aspects of the text was very limited – well below the range for his actual age. His teacher had also noticed that John was often left out of group games in the playground and found great difficulty managing the small group activities organised in class. She and the previous class teacher noted that John found it impossible to cope with the increasingly abstract requirements of some of the curriculum. In comprehension, for example, despite his superb spelling and excellent textual recall, he could not answer questions like, 'What do you think the boy did next?' or 'How do you think he felt when . . . ?' In short, John provided a puzzling picture that had taken his teachers some time to feel concerned about. His remarkable talents in some areas had masked his increasing difficulties in abstract thinking (Piaget 1954), social discourse, the capacity to feel and show a wide range of emotions (Freud 1966) and a capacity to learn new things. He was also physically awkward and uncoordinated.

In discussing John with his parents, it was clear that they also had concerns and had found him puzzling and 'a bit odd'. Only recently, though, had it become so evident that he was in some measure different from other children in the way he thought and related. A likeable child, he clearly enjoyed school and participating in normal school life. Yet a period of observation showed that he tended to work either alone or, occasionally, in a pair with one other boy, his best friend. He could not manage small groupwork as he would always want to be the one talking or doing something, and he had very little tolerance of any limitations shown by other children. Furthermore, his social interactions tended to be naive, inappropriate and almost exclusively self-centred. For example, failing to pick up social cues about when to start or stop a communication or indeed how to engage other people, he would spend ages telling another boy, in great detail, about a film he had seen, regardless of whether that boy had seen the film himself or was showing any interest.

Thinking with John

I began to work with John in his classroom because his teachers, parents and I believed that John would find the intensity of individual contact on a withdrawal basis intimidating. Indeed, when I did venture to try this later, John found the experience frightening, confirming my view that he needed an intervention designed specifically to help him develop certain social skills and learning tools that would better enable him to take part in school life. My intervention was also diagnostic, and on the basis of the work, John was referred to specialist provision to help him manage his social and communication difficulties.

I worked with John individually at times, at others with one or two other children as well. During the first few months, sessions with John were often like battlegrounds, as he fought to maintain absolute control of events. For example, he manoeuvred himself so that there was no space for me to sit beside him, forcing me to sit behind him or on the other side of the table. This behaviour felt as if a physical barrier was being put between us; a wall that he did not want breached at any cost. His attitude towards me was dismissive and contemptuous. He loved to point out any mistakes I made and would triumphantly point these out to others. Extremely resistant to any help I offered, for some months he seemed stuck in a pattern of repetitive, obsessional behaviour – for example, copying texts from draft into neat copy, completing pages of sums that presented no challenge to him, reading book after book with no apparent comprehension of the story-line.

At times, when I was with John, I found myself gripped by feelings of anger and a wish to control him in rather a punitive, even cruel manner. I also felt grossly inadequate as I recoiled from his exacting memory and his delight in ruthlessly pointing out my slightest limitation. These countertransference feelings helped me understand more about John's view of others, of relationships and of himself. In my view, John had developed around him a shield which protected him from the apparent terrors of separation and the conflict inherent in recognising the differences between people. This shield had been an essential factor in supporting John during his early years at school, allowing him to be seen as an unusual child and bright enough to cope with the curricula. However, on reaching the last years of his primary school, John's shield was no longer adequate to keep his limitations out of sight.

During one of John's early sessions with me, he began to draw a picture of Thomas the Tank Engine. In silence, he drew Thomas puffing along a track towards a large notice proclaiming, 'STOP! Do not go beyond this point!' Puzzling about the meaning of this, I asked John to tell me what Thomas might do next. John announced, with absolute certainty and a sense of urgency, that Thomas *must* stop. He must *not* go on. Beyond this point lay a dangerous abyss, a hole. Further, Thomas must *not* go off the rails. He had to stick to the lines, otherwise he would be exposed to other dangers. Thomas could only go back or stay at this point. This session alerted me to John's anxiety about my arrival and what I might do with him. In time, it became clearer that John was frightened about the prospects of engaging with me in a process of learning that, inevitably challenging his view of the world, might force him to 'go beyond [that] point' which marked the limit of his feeling of safety.

Ostensibly, my task was to try and help John find new ways of approaching learning so that he could keep up with the increasing demands of the curricula as he approached his last year in primary school. I addressed this task by letting John show me what he felt comfortable doing. I was working towards helping John to feel safe enough to let me be someone to whom he could reveal his limitations, his fears about uncertainty and not knowing. I hoped John might develop a wider range of responses to situations that challenged his need for omnipotent control.

My entrée into making contact with John – reaching beyond this shield-like presentation – occurred accidentally. I happened to take off my glasses to clean them and I became aware of John's attention focused on me. John was looking into my eyes with the kind of intensity that I have only experienced with babies. This look carried with it the suggestion that I was being reached into, right inside; seen, as it were, to the core. This moment seemed to hold John and me still for what seemed a long time but was only seconds; I without my shield and John without his. After this, John gazed at me often, sometimes asking me to look at him and to take off my glasses. I recall finding these occasions extremely moving, evoking a wealth of feelings, often contradictory ones like affection and irritation, much as a mother might feel in relation to her child. I found myself reminded of Trevarthen's (1979) phrase, 'companion in experience' and Schaffer's (1977) idea that the 'mother's gaze following her baby's gaze helps his thoughts become thinkable and be lent meaning that is shared in time and through time'.

I felt that this was an extremely significant phase in helping John and I to work together. I suggest that, in some way, John felt held by the fact that I could survive his emotional intensity without my glasses or shield, and that this experience of life outside the constraints within which he normally operated, contributed to helping him explore ways of relating to others in safety.

Following this phase, we were able to begin the very slow process of trying to establish a relationship in which he could begin to feel secure enough to allow himself to venture beyond the rigid patterns that he had constructed. He made considerable progress over time, so that when we parted, he had managed to make forays into the kind of social interaction that was more like that of his peers, to develop a greater capacity to generalise and thus problem solve and, perhaps most importantly, to be less reluctant to show his feelings towards me and others. Indeed, during our last six months, it seemed as though John was practising a range of ways of expressing his feelings, particularly aggression and affection.

Conclusion

In order to learn in a school context, a child needs to have internalised a benign and thoughtful figure who, by repeatedly containing his or her unbearable feelings and representing them in a meaningful form, enables the child to feel safe enough to cope thoughtfully with the emotional demands of development and the learning that this involves. In my experience, some children referred to the learning support service do not feel safe enough to learn. These children need individual help, characterised by the capacity for holding and containment, to facilitate the developmental moves necessary for enabling them to take an active part in the social and learning environment of the school.

I suggest that the conditions required to help these children feel safe can be generalised to all children and, furthermore, applied to the contribution made by the wider systems of classroom and school. Here I concur with the view that 'Special educational needs are not just a reflection of pupils' inherent difficulties; they are often related to factors within schools which can prevent or exacerbate some problems' (NCC 1989, No. 5).

Children who communicate their anxieties about learning are disturbing, for, unconsciously and too painfully, they can remind teachers and other staff of their own difficulties as learners. It is worth noting here the valuable work done by Salzberger-Wittenberg *et al.* (1983) on the emotional difficulties experienced by adults in a learning situation. The authors draw upon the experience of teachers to illustrate, most evocatively, the mental pain and ensuing anxieties associated with learning. These anxieties are: 'fear of confusion and chaos in the face of unsorted "bricks" of experience, helplessness in the face of not knowing, fear of inadequacy, fear of being judged stupid in comparison with others' (ibid: 1983: 57). In the context of schooling, it is the task of teachers to accommodate this kind of mental pain and mediate what might feel quite unbearable to some pupils in the hope that learning may take place. 'Real learning and discovery can only take place when a state of not knowing can be borne for long enough to enable all the data gathered by the senses to be taken in and explored until some meaningful pattern emerges' (ibid. 1983: 58).

Unfortunately, in my experience, the difficulties and pleasures inherent in the learning situation, for both pupils and teachers, are often glossed over and minimised. I suggest that teachers can only be expected to manage the emotional and organisational complexities of teaching if they are working in an environment that makes provision for them to both have individual time for reflection and the opportunity to meet regularly with colleagues (see Hanko 1990). By drawing attention to this significant limitation, I emphasise the crucial role played by emotional life in both learning and teaching processes.

Notes

1 I use the present tense when talking about this work, though this is no longer my role.
2 Statutory provision for a child on the basis of a multidisciplinary assessment of educational need.

References

Advisory Centre for Education (ACE) (1989) 'A National Curriculum for all – the rights of children and their parents under Section 19 of the Education Reform Act: temporary exceptions from the National Curriculum', Conference, 4 October.

Bion, W. R. (1962) *Learning from Experience*, London: William Heinemann Medical Books.

Bowlby, J. (1978) *Attachment: Attachment and Loss: Volume 1*, Harmondsworth: Penguin Books.

Bruner, J. (1960) *The Process of Education*, Cambridge, MA: Harvard University Press.

Department of Education and Science (DES) (1978) *Special Educational Needs (Warnock Report)*, Cmnd 7212 , London: HMSO.

—— (1988) *Education Reform Act*, London: DES.

Figlio, K. (1991) 'The future of analytical psychotherapy: what do we profess?', *Free Associations*, Vol. 4, Pt 1: No. 29.

Freud, A. (1966) *Normality and Pathology in Childhood*, London: Penguin Books, 1973.

Hanko, G. (1990) *Special Needs in Ordinary Classrooms: Supporting Teachers*, London: Blackwell.

Klein, M. (1921) 'The development of a child', in *Love, Guilt and Reparation (1921–1945)*, London: Hogarth Press.

National Curriculum Council (NCC) (1989) *Circular 5: Implementing the National Curriculum – Participation by Pupils with Special Educational Needs*, York.

Piaget, J. (1954) *Construction of Reality in the Child*, London: Routledge & Kegan Paul.

Salzberger-Wittenberg, I., Henry, G. and Osborne, E. (1983) *The Emotional Experience of Learning and Teaching*, London and New York: Routledge.

Schaffer, H. (1977) *Studies in Mother–Infant Interaction*, London: Academic Press.

Trevarthen, C. (1979) 'Communication and cooperation in early infancy: a description of primary inter subjectivity', in M. M. Bullowa (ed.), *Before Speech: The Beginning of Interpersonal Communication*, New York: Cambridge University Press.

Winnicott, D. W. (1946) 'Some psychological aspects of juvenile delinquency', in *The Child and the Outside World: Studies in Developing Relationships*, London: Tavistock, 1957.

—— (1960) 'The theory of the parent–infant relationship', in *The Maturational Process and the Facilitating Environment*, London: Hogarth Press, 1965.

—— (1975) *Through Paediatrics To Psycho-Analysis*, London: The Hogarth Press and the Institute of Psycho-Analysis.

Chapter 6

Combining teacher and therapist roles
Making the space and taming the dragon

Sarah Adams

Introduction

> Once there was a little boy who sat on a swing and did somersaults.
> One day he did a somersault and was turned inside out so that his
> heart was on the outside and from then on he was called the 'inside-
> out-boy'. After several fights he got back on the swing and doing a
> backwards somersault he became a normal boy again.

Daniel recounted this dream shortly after he had arrived at 'The Lodge',
a special school for primary age children who have emotional and
behavioural difficulties. It was in essence Daniel's greatest wish; a
symbolic representation of his journey towards a more positive future –
towards emotional integration – when his heart could find itself back on
the inside.

Daniel's means of coping with the pain in his life was to keep moving,
to jump, run, somersault, anything which would stop him from feeling
the hurt or thinking about it. In the classroom, he could not concentrate
or sit still for long enough to take anything in. He was already 'full up' with
anxiety and fear. Having been rejected by his mother he had to keep
everyone at a distance. To allow anyone close would be to acknowledge
the loss of his mother and the pain this caused him. Daniel was not
unintelligent, but by the age of nine he had lost the capacity to think, to
absorb, to learn. A consequence of finding his heart back on the inside
would be for Daniel to once again be able to access the learning process.

All children who arrive at 'The Lodge' have their own dreams and
stories. Their stories, often about rejection, abandonment, violence or
abuse are traumatic, sad and painful. The defences employed by these
children mean that they are insecure, unhappy and often unable to form
meaningful relationships with peers or adults. They can evoke in those

trying to teach them strong feelings of despair, frustration and confusion; feelings, which if not understood and managed, can lead the adult to react in ways which only serve to reinforce the strong messages already received by the child.

Common to all these children is the difficulty which learning presents. Preoccupied with overwhelming anxiety and insecurity, which makes the world a precarious place, the fragmented child cannot trust his environment or those within it enough to begin to explore it further. Until a child has experienced an emotional environment which can facilitate exploration, his hope of becoming integrated remains tenuous and fragile. In other words, before a child can begin to access the learning environment, he first needs to experience a positive attachment.

It is an understanding of attachment theory in particular which has helped the staff of 'The Lodge' to formulate their ideas and practice; to begin to make sense of the muddled and confused communications of the children who come into their classrooms. This chapter sets out to show how the school works within an attachment framework, how this framework enables me (a class teacher and drama therapist) to offer individual therapy and how, through such therapy, children may confront and challenge their behaviour in a way that makes them better able to explore and learn.

Understanding attachment theory

Attachment theory (Bowlby 1969) focuses on the oscillation between the need for security and the need to explore. When tiredness, illness, hunger, strangers or darkness dominate, a child seeks out an attachment figure (e.g. mother) to assuage his anxiety and distress. The mother's ability to respond to this distress determines the child's capacity to feel secure. Only if he feels secure will his natural capacity to be curious develop. Only if he has the capacity to be curious will he be moved to explore.

The activity of exploration implies both the possession of a 'secure base' (Ainsworth et al. 1978; Bowlby 1988) from which to explore and the willingness to separate from that base. The available mother enables her child to tolerate separation because her responsiveness allows him a secure memory of safety; of feeling states reflected, of anxieties ameliorated and contained (Bion 1962; see also chapters 1, 5 and 11). As confidence in safety increases, the perceived risk of danger decreases. Thus the child is free to explore other people and situations knowing that his mother will be there when he needs her. The certain knowledge of a reliable attachment figure who can think through anxieties, provide succour, offer safety, is also gradually internalised, so that to some degree and for increasing periods of time the child comes to trust these capacities within himself. Such trust releases him from constant anxious scrutiny of his external environment and enables him to feel safe enough to concentrate, to reflect and to play alone.

The child's exploratory behaviour seems to begin as he becomes more responsive through smiling and vocalisations, developing later to crawling, walking and exploration of the immediate environment. This process actively continues as such behaviour is encouraged within acceptable setting of boundaries which protect the child as well as introducing him to the concept that another person may have a different goal to his own. The secure child will carry this process into school. As a securely attached child grows up, he is constantly in the process of what Bowlby (1988) refers to as 'updating' his internal working model. It is through this process of updating and adjusting the manner of interacting with others that the skills for creative play and cognitive learning are also developed (Barrett and Trevitt 1991).

When it has not been possible for the mother to be emotionally available to her child in this way, the child's anxious feelings regarding the absence of an attachment figure will take precedence over his desire and willingness to explore. In the same way, the mother who is inconsistent, threatening or who discourages proximity can elicit intensely anxious attachment behaviour. This then stops the child wanting to separate and explore. Bowlby also suggests that unprepared-for separations can have the same impact.

Children who have not been able to develop a secure attachment are either avoidant or ambivalent. The child who is avoidant appears happy to be left with a stranger, and either avoids or rejects the mother when she approaches following a separation. Already he is unable to express one of his deepest feelings (e.g. fear) or his need for comfort and assurance which accompanies it. The ambivalent or resistant child, on the other hand, is intensely upset by separation but, when mother returns, seems ambivalent. He wants to be close but is also angry and difficult to soothe. Such children find it difficult to return to play and will resist being put down. Mothers of these children have been observed as being inconsistent in their behaviour towards their child.

The anxiously attached child is one who remains in a state of uncertainty about his relationship with an attachment figure. As a result, it is unlikely that Bowlby's concept of a healthy internal working model has developed and thus 'updating' exists in a negative form. As a consequence, his feelings about himself in his interaction with attachment figures are transferred to his teachers. He sees himself as 'bad' or 'useless', has low self-esteem and difficulties in managing his behaviour and feelings. There is often a sense of 'self-fulfilling prophecy' as he sets out to prove to others that he is as he perceives himself to be. Each time the experience is repeated, the child's inner representation of how he interacts is confirmed. It takes consistently different and positive messages to change these perceptions and for positive 'updating' to be enabled.

Theory in context

From home to school

When the securely attached child makes the transition from home to school, he will have already experienced predictable responses and an environment which is flexible to change and tolerant to different moods. The anxiously attached child, however, will not be able to predict his or others' behaviour. He will find exploration difficult and put much energy into being close to a primary care giver either by rejecting or clinging behaviour.

Patrick, a nine year old, is one example of such a child. He lived at home with his mother, father and younger brothers of five and three. He had experienced several periods of hospitalisation as a baby, had difficulty feeding (refusing milk) and as a toddler was referred to the occupational therapist for motor coordination difficulties. On referral to 'The Lodge' at the age of six, Patrick was underweight and small for his age. He had many cuts and sores on his body as a result of permanently picking at his skin until it bled. This he had done from the time he was a baby.

Patrick was referred to the school because of poor motor skills, lack of concentration and aggressive behaviour. His behaviour was unpredictable and obsessive. He often refused food and, if he did eat, he would then make himself sick. He would only eat a particular variety of meat but this also depended on his mood. On one occasion he refused to eat anything because there was a mark on his shirt. When his mother had insisted he wear the shirt, he had told her he would not eat his lunch that day because she would not change it.

It seemed that Patrick's obsessive behaviour, self-mutilation and inability to express any feelings (he was always 'happy' and often had a fixed smile) were manifestations of an anxiety attachment. There was often a sense of Patrick needing to control his environment while at the same time experiencing an inner chaos of confused feelings. A consequence of this was Patrick's fear of learning. Any new task filled him with anxiety. He needed to have an adult continually by his side and the lack of one resulted in stubborn, obsessive behaviour, such as picking at his mouth and fingers until they bled, or insisting that other children had taken his belongings, resulting in him physically attacking them while squealing loudly. These behaviours, among others, would inevitably see the return of an adult to his side, thus overcoming the inner sense of 'falling apart', a fragmenting which he seemed to experience in the absence of an attachment figure.

The level of anxiety within Patrick meant that any new situation in the classroom evoked a sense of panic. Presenting him with something new required us to prepare him for the transition from something familiar to something unfamiliar. It was crucial to support him in this to prevent his overwhelming anxiety from dominating his thoughts and behaviour. Within the context of a mainstream classroom, Patrick's fear could not be readily assuaged, causing him to react in the only way he knew how, by ensuring his presence was keenly felt (e.g. loud screaming, attacking others, etc.). Only after eighteen months of working with Patrick, during which time he had moved into the class taught by myself and another female teacher, did his behaviour slowly begin to change. Although we rarely taught the class together, our methods ensured that the children experienced consistency across the week. It was as if the children experienced us as 'one'. Although we taught different areas of the curriculum, the beginning and the ending of the day remained the same. In addition, we approached our lessons with a similar structure which became familiar to the children. We communicated regularly with each other, 'thinking' about the children and struggling together to understand the children's inner worlds as well as their presenting behaviours.

Our way of working was supported by the whole school approach, which centred on providing an environment which was predictable and secure. Each moment of the day was thought about from the time the children arrived in the morning until they left in the afternoon. The daily staff meeting at the end of the day, when the behaviour and progress of each child was discussed, helped to focus the thinking of the staff and consider their own responses and feelings in relation to the children for whom they were responsible. The capacity of the staff group to understand a child's behaviour as a form of communication enabled them to be less reactive and more reflective in their responses. The headteacher maintained a total non-exclusion policy based on the belief that the children who came to the school had already experienced significant rejection and needed to experience a group of adults who could 'hold' (see

Chapter 2), contain and survive the deep rage and despair they projected. A combination of this policy and the support then offered to everyone within the school enabled the adults to focus on the children and to feel contained within themselves.

In addition to the continual thinking and absorbing of behaviour which went on, there was a belief that the children would only change their behaviour if they could change the image they had of themselves. To this end, a positive reinforcement working policy was implemented. Achievement was recognised and acknowledged and, as far as possible, negative behaviour was ignored or at least thought about with the child. Through a containing, non-judgemental approach in which the boundaries were made very clear, Patrick began to experience an environment which was predictable and consistent, where adults were available to him and able to absorb and make sense of the strong feelings he projected. The absorbing and making sense of Patrick's painful feelings enabled him to experience them as more bearable. He became more willing to work independently and allowed himself to make mistakes which in earlier months he could not tolerate. He continued to have difficulty expressing his feelings but his fixed smile began to disappear and he was able to cry. He still found it difficult to name his feelings however and, even when crying, he would say, 'I'm happy'. What specifically changed was Patrick's academic progress. He became a confident reader and went from a reading age of 5.3 to 9.6 in eighteen months. At playtime he would allow himself to leave his teacher's side for several minutes before running back to her, checking that she was still there.

Clinical work

From classroom to therapy

The containing nature of both the classroom and the school made offering individual and group therapy a natural part of the life of 'The Lodge'. However, as both a teacher and therapist, I needed to be confident that therapy was not seen as an added extra but as an integral part of a child's programme within the school. The provision of any form of therapy within a school setting can be fraught with difficulties, not least being the provision of a regular time and space which allows for work to take place consistently and without interruption. In addition, the issue of confidentiality, crucial to the therapeutic relationship, can be a thorny one within a school where information can be seen to be the domain of all. 'The Lodge', however, was respectful of these issues since the approach to all aspects of the school day was considered within a therapeutic framework. Thus a room was set aside which was ideal for individual drama and play therapy.

Confidentiality was respected in relation to the content of the session, while general issues and themes which emerged could be thought about by the staff group within the context of termly reviews which were held for each child. It should be noted that, within the area of confidentiality, it was made clear to children that all staff were available to talk to about anything in confidence. However, if the content of such a conversation suggested that the child or anyone else was at risk, confidentiality could not be guaranteed. The children appeared to accept this and to understand that it was their safety and well-being which was the concern of the staff.

These safety issues of time, space and confidentiality were the easiest areas to establish when setting up therapy in the school. The most difficult hurdle, as I saw it, was whether or not the children would accept my change in role from teacher to therapist and be able to trust the different nature of our relationship. Within any therapeutic relationship the establishment of trust takes time, but I had the added dimension of seeing children on a daily basis and in a role of authority. If I reacted badly to a situation within the classroom how would the child then experience me within the therapy room? The thinking I engaged in gave me a clarity about what I was offering and why. For me, this individual time with a child was about offering an intensive experience of what was already provided in the classroom. Key areas related to establishing a safe and containing space where feelings and thoughts could be expressed freely. There was a clear structure to the sessions (i.e. a clear beginning and ending); behaviour and feelings were reflected on and it was made clear that what took place in the sessions would not be referred to outside of the therapy room.

The child was assured that, within therapy, I was not expecting him to achieve a particular result as I might in the classroom, where, as his teacher, I was concerned with his learning progress and, wanting him to achieve, would help him in particular tasks in order to do so. In therapy, by contrast, the focus was on him learning about himself, in his own time and at his own pace. As his therapist, I would be there to support him by listening to and exploring with him his own thoughts, ideas and feelings.

Making the transition to and from a therapy session was important to consider. To facilitate this, therapy was timetabled on a day when I did not teach and when I did not have to engage in playground duties. In this way, I was able to focus specifically on therapy and be separate from the daily running of my class. Children were brought to me by a classroom assistant and collected by the same person at the end of the session. By including all staff in the thinking about how therapy would be offered, I ensured that they had some understanding of the therapeutic process. It was important that this transition period was not accompanied by a cacophony of exhortations and questions on the part of the adult, such as 'Make sure you behave' or 'Did you have a good time?' However well intentioned such comments may be, they can give the child confused messages about what therapy is.

With the children, I made it clear that they could choose what they did with me but they could not hurt me or themselves, or damage property. This was different to the behaviour allowed around the school, where there were certain rules (albeit few) which had to be maintained. It was interesting to note that the child who might swear profusely in therapy would often cease to swear in the classroom. I would not comment on this difference in either therapy or the classroom, but it served to demonstrate for me a child's confidence in the safety of the therapy room as well as their ability to use language appropriately.

Ultimately, what seemed to help the children in accepting me in both roles was my clarity about the difference between roles and my consistency within them. Children have to experience something consistently before they will begin to accept that adults mean what they say and they can begin to trust what is happening.

Clinical work

Using metaphor

As a Sesame[1] trained drama and movement therapist (see Pearson 1996), I offer a creative space within a structured framework where feelings and emotions can be explored through the use of metaphor. Stories are a powerful medium in this process. Since children who have experienced difficult and traumatic early beginnings often struggle to verbalise what has happened to them, they will find other ways of 'coping' with the pain. In Jungian terms, this can lead to a locking away of the parts of ourselves that do not fit in with how we wish or others wish us to be. Jung (1958) believed that it is this locking away within our unconscious which creates the shadow parts of ourselves; this is where the witches, ogres, monsters and dragons of fairy stories reside. To be truly ourselves, we have to reclaim these aspects of ourselves and integrate them within our conscious self. If we do not integrate these parts they are likely to emerge when we least expect them, often detrimentally to our relationships.

The use of the art-forms, particularly myth, legend and fairy-tale, allow an indirect approach or access to the difficulty; an oblique route to the dragons and monsters within (see Bettelheim 1975). Giving children the opportunity to choose and enact roles within such stories provides a way of dealing with problems that cannot be faced confrontationally. In addition, a story provides a container. Just as the mother who, in tune with her baby's feeling state, is able to accept the feelings projected into her, make sense of them and return them to her baby in a form which he can tolerate, so too the story acts as a vessel which holds and gives form to all kinds of feelings which can then be made sense of and expressed safely. The structure of a story, with its beginning, middle and end, adds to this sense of a containing, boundaried space in which a child, enacting his chosen roles, can play (Winnicott 1971).

Jason

Jason was a very disturbed seven year old. Hospitalisation as a baby, major brain surgery and later, the loss of a baby sister as a result of cot death, left him with a strong need to be in control of his environment and his feelings. For example, in therapy, whenever he enacted a story, he insisted on using flowery, dramatic language, even though he struggled to follow the sequence of the story presented. He often became confused or muddled. Yet the greater his muddle and confusion, the louder and more dramatic he became. In his wider environment, his need for control seemed to indicate the *avoidant* nature of his attachment difficulties. He would happily greet strangers and, without request, take them on guided tours around the school. However, to his peers and teachers – those who offered more constant and potentially closer attachments – he was frequently hostile. His cruelty towards other children and his refusal to comply with rules left him socially isolated; an isolation that appeared to stem from his feelings of omnipotence (see Chapter 5), and what he feared was an unbounded capacity for destructiveness. This capacity appeared to him to be confirmed by the death of his baby sister whose presence in the family he had resented and who, unconsciously, he believed he had killed off.

The provision of individual drama therapy sessions seemed to provide Jason with a safe, containing space where eventually he was able to express some feelings. The work was clearly structured and the beginning of the session soon became ritualistic. I adopted a greeting gesture (a Japanese-style bow) which initially Jason had mockingly introduced. His surprise that I had accepted it allowed him to repeat it with confidence and seriousness thereafter. We then expressed how we felt by a gesture with the body, eventually adding a sound to go with it. At the outset, Jason was unable to use an appropriate word to express such feelings but, through this approach, we gradually began to find such words as 'happy', 'sad' and 'angry'.

During the session we moved to mirroring each other's movements using gentle music in the background and extended this to making contrasting movements. Through the latter, Jason began to find a flow in his body which was less rigid, although at times it could feel competitive. We would make forests and caves and rocks together, depending on the content of the story to come. With Jason I used many fairy-tales; *Beauty and the Beast* and *The Snow Queen* were his favourites. It was always necessary to break the story down into simple sections for Jason to hold the story-line, but his self esteem began to grow as he achieved this. As time passed, he became less controlling and more able to negotiate. *The Caterpillar and the Wild Animals*, a Masai myth of Africa (see Gersie and King 1990), seemed to be the turning point in helping Jason with the belief he held that somehow his wishful thinking had killed his baby sister. In the story, the caterpillar claims to be monstrous, 'all powerful'. 'I am the great warrior,' he says, 'who can crush elephants and turn rhinoceros to dust. I am invincible.' All the animals are terrified of the caterpillar (who is hiding in Hare's house and cannot be seen) until Frog takes a huge breath and shouts back even more loudly. When Caterpillar hears Frog's ferocious voice he crawls out, saying, 'Do not hurt me. I am only a caterpillar.' The animals laugh when they realise the trick he has played on them.

Jason's inner fear was that he had killed off his baby sister by wishing her dead. The reality of her death served to corroborate his sense of omnipotence which could never be challenged directly. Through the role of the caterpillar, Jason seemed able to express this sense of omnipotence, experience the power it had over others but then be able to acknowledge that he was not so powerful. Caterpillar had tricked the animals but they laughed. Caterpillar was not destroyed by being 'found out'.

Jason asked for this story several sessions in a row. Together we would play out the different roles but always, at some point, Jason took on the role of the caterpillar. As the sessions progressed, we were able to talk about how Caterpillar might feel in the belief that he had all that monstrous power and wonder about what might have happened if Frog had not challenged his thinking/feeling. Prior to this story we had used *Aladdin's Lamp*, and Jason asked me if I thought that if we wished for something very hard, could it come true? My response was to reflect back to him that perhaps, sometimes, he would like his wishes to come true but that, at other times, when things he wished for did come true, it was very frightening.

Although Jason's excessive need to control his environment did not go away entirely, it did diminish. As we moved on from the story of the caterpillar, Jason's concerns about wishes and thinking things which then happened no longer seemed so important. Within the classroom, Jason's need to create a disturbance to avoid his work gave way to a greater willingness in asking for help and letting it be known that he was confused or did not understand. His trust in the environment and the teacher became less fragile as he became more secure in the knowledge that he was safe and not 'all-powerful' and that he no longer needed to maintain the guise of some monstrous dragon. Meanwhile, in his story writing, he began to have a sense of structure and to remember the order of events correctly.

William

William, an eight year old, was referred to the school at the age of five for bizarre and disruptive behaviour. He was described as a loner, at times a bit of a monster, who was unable to relate to other children. Referring to himself as 'William', he seemed to have no sense of himself as 'I'. He wandered around the school sucking two fingers and, though he liked to be close to adults, he was aggressive and threatening. At home, he craved the attention of his mother who seemed ambivalent in her feelings towards him. Often William's attempts to cuddle up to her, especially when his younger sister was around, were met with rejection – she would push him away. At other times she spoke of great fondness for him, but found it difficult to express this physically. William was intensely jealous of his younger sibling.

When William first came to the class he was extremely loud and flamboyant in his behaviour, often strutting around the room flailing his arms about, and very resistant to boundaries. He regularly threatened to bring relatives to school to 'beat me up'. As time passed he stopped this behaviour and began to settle in the classroom. However, he frequently followed me around school, asking me where I was going and, usually on a Friday or as holidays approached, whether I would take him home with me. In this way, William showed himself to be extremely affectionate, craving physical contact as might a baby. When working with him he would want to sit on my lap and he often looked for hugs. At the same time, however, typical of an *ambivalently attached* child, he expressed his affection aggressively, trying to pull me over or push me away.

As the year progressed, William was more able to work independently, but he continued to drift at playtimes, often playing alone, two fingers in his mouth. His handwriting in particular seemed to emphasise his need for attachment and his fear of separation. He would write long paragraphs of sentences which were made up of words joined together; (e.g. 'Thesunsetwasveryred'). Despite attempts to help him to space his words, he found it very difficult, and became angry and distressed when help was offered. As a consequence of his behaviour, the difficulties he experienced with learning (he hated anything new) and his poor self-esteem, we decided to offer him individual drama therapy in addition to the drama therapy in a class context.

The aim of the sessions was to provide William with a sense of himself in relation to others, and for him to begin to negotiate separation and loss. William's difficulties with transitions stemmed from an attachment experience which had not allowed for separation. His mother's inconsistent responses to him as a baby and throughout his childhood had, it seemed, created within him a fear of the world which made him both desperate for closeness and terrified of contact. Having failed to internalise a mother readily available to him, he could not begin to feel safe enough to leave her and explore his environment. This sense of having to hold on to himself, in isolation from others, manifested itself in his need to suck his fingers and wander around alone, adrift in his 'own world'.

For William to make progress, it seemed crucial that he be given the opportunity to develop an attachment with an appropriate adult who could, in turn, allow him the opportunity to experience separation in a way which would not leave him feeling abandoned. It was hoped that this would enable him to develop a positive sense of himself, thus allowing him to relate to his peers in a meaningful way. (At the time, his only way of communicating with them was to hit them and then run away.)

Within the sessions, my awareness of these aims led me to choose stories which contained themes of journey, time, beginnings and endings. I hoped that this kind of material, in addition to the therapeutic relationship, would offer him the chance to explore his feelings of insecurity, his fear of the world and those around him.

During the first sessions William was hesitant, awkward and at times difficult to engage. As time passed, he participated with greater enthusiasm, adding his own elements to the story. Around the school, he became increasingly 'clingy' towards me and I had to be very sensitive about how I responded to this, so that William neither felt rejected nor my possession. On these occasions, I would try to reflect back what seemed to be his feeling state at the time. Very often, commenting on the fact that he was there was enough to enable him to go off again. On other occasions, when he seemed particularly clingy, I wondered aloud why this might be and allowed him to remain at my side by engaging him in an activity with me which ensured that others were not excluded.

The change for William seemed to come in the third term of therapy when we enacted an Australian Dreamtime story of a frog, Tiddalik, who drinks all the water (see Gersie 1992). The other animals have to persuade Tiddalik to laugh so that he will release the water before they die. I chose this story because there was a strong theme within it about holding on and letting go. There was a sense for me that William's fear of losing made him cling on and never want to let go. I hoped that William might experience letting go as freeing rather than something which led to destruction or collapse. William chose to play the frog. When it came to trying to make Tiddalik laugh, William held himself tightly, maintained a serious expression and refused to laugh. When we reached the point in the story when Tiddalik does laugh, William let out a roar and really did laugh.

In the weeks which followed, it was notable that William seemed calmer, less clinging and more able to work on his own. Many of his stories became easier to read because he began to separate his words. At the same time, he began to make friends with another child. Although he continued to express anxiety with approaching weekends and holidays, this was to a lesser degree. He continued to ask me to take him home but with less despair in his voice. There was a sense that within the secure base of the classroom, alongside that of a containing drama therapy session, William was able to renegotiate very early attachment experiences and to begin to develop a more integrated sense of himself. He was able to experience an attachment figure who was consistent in her responses and able to contain his difficult feelings. Often evoking in me feelings of frustration, sadness and despair, I knew I had to absorb, make sense of and return these feelings to him in a way which left him feeling emotionally held.

It seemed that William had not experienced adults who could see his loud and flamboyant aggression as an expression of his fear. Instead, he was accustomed to being told off or shouted at – thus the dragon grew larger within. By trying to make sense of what he was actually communicating, he experienced an attachment figure who was consistent in her responses and able to contain his difficult feelings. As a consequence, like Tiddalik, William was able to 'let go' and be separate. The significance of this was apparent when he stopped referring to himself as 'William' and was able to say 'I'.

Conclusion

In all of us, there is a story; a story which lies at the heart of us; a story which needs time and space for the sharing of experience before it can be told. The opportunity for children to begin to tell their story through individual drama therapy has not only proved valuable in its own right, but has enhanced the process of learning development to which 'The Lodge' is committed.

In the story of St George and the Dragon, George has a quest. It is a search for health and happiness – the Holy Grail. Before George can achieve this, he must first slay the dragon. For Jason, William and those children who have suffered the real-life injuries of abuse and trauma, neglect and/or loss, although the monstrous dragon, like St George's, stands between them and health and happiness, it cannot and should not be slain. Rather, its roar needs to be heard and understood as the defensive posturing of the vulnerable caterpillar, as the distressed cry of the uncertain, anxious, insecurely attached child. The dragon parts of these children's selves must have their space, but they must not be allowed to dominate, to run wild. Instead, they need to be reclaimed and integrated. Gradually, by naming the darkness within and beginning to make sense of the pain, the child may begin to tame the dragon and, securing a lead around its neck, put it behind him.

By combining the role of teacher and therapist, I am allowed a greater degree of understanding and insight into the inner world of the children with whom I work. My observations of them in the classroom and playground, not normally accessible to the therapist, give me a broader sense of their difficulties, and an understanding which I am able to hold in mind within therapy. Equally, the insights I gain by seeing a child in therapy provide me with clues about what might be going on in the classroom and the impact it might be having on the learning task.

What is important in both roles is the capacity to think about the child, to hold him in mind and to be experienced by the child as an adult who is consistently available to him in an emotional sense. The capacity to do this requires me to have a strong sense of my own emotional world and a supervisor who can help me make sense of the child's struggle, separate to my own.

Note

1   Sesame is a charitable organisation which provides a one-year full-time postgraduate training course in conjunction with the Central School of Speech and Drama, London.

References

Ainsworth, M. D., Blehar, M., Waters, E. and Wall, S. (1978) *Patterns of Attachment: Assessed in the Strange Situation and at Home*, Hillsdale, NJ: Erlbaum.

Barrett, M. and Trevitt, J. (1991) *Attachment Behaviour and the School Child*, London: Routledge.

Bettelheim, B. (1975) *Uses of Enchantment*, London: Penguin Books.

Bion, W. (1962) *Learning from Experience*, London: Heinemann/Karnac, 1984.

Bowlby, J. (1969) *Attachment and Loss Vol. 1, Attachment*, London: Hogarth Press.

—— (1988) *A Secure Base: Clinical Applications of Attachment Theory*, London: Tavistock.

Gersie, A. (1992) *Earth Tales*, Green Print.

Gersie, A. and King, N. (1990) *Storymaking in Education and Therapy*, London: Jessica Kingsley.

Jung, C. G. (1958) *Collected Works Vol. II. Psychology and Religion*, London: Routledge.

Pearson, J. (ed.) (1996) *Discovering the Self through Drama and Movement; The Sesame Approach*, London: Jessica Kingsley.

Winnicott, D. W. (1971) *Playing and Reality*, London: Penguin Books.

Chapter 7

The use of cognitive-behavioural therapy for counselling in schools

June Platts and Yuki Williamson[1]

Introduction

It is as true with children as it is with adults, that an emotional disturbance in one area of their lives will affect them in other areas of their lives. School thus becomes the battleground for many non-school-related problems as well as school-associated ones. This chapter explores the rationale behind cognitive-behavioural therapy (CBT) and shows how, by using CBT techniques to identify, challenge and change distorted or maladaptive thoughts, beliefs and behaviours, some children are able to reverse the slow (or sometimes fast) slide towards academic failure, exclusion or removal to a special school. Because of the formally structured style of CBT, which mirrors many of the familiar structures of school, the particular appropriateness of the CBT approach as a method of counselling in schools will also be considered.

Meeting the demands of the context

Most of my working life has been spent as part of a multidisciplinary team in a child and family psychiatric service and, although my original training was psychodynamic, it became more and more clear to me that, on their own and within the time available, psychodynamic counselling skills were not enough to effect real change. This was particularly so when working with children who could not conform at school or home, many of whom came to us as a last resort and often after waiting some time for an appointment. These children presented with a wide range of difficulties, from anxiety to depression, from conduct disorder to school refusal, from violent or emotional outbursts to school-based masturbatory activities. I needed to be able to offer effective strategies to help them, that could be seen to be working and that could be explained to parents and teachers as well as the child. So I trained as a cognitive-behavioural psychotherapist.

Cognitive-behavioural therapy, with its emphasis on developing effective strategies to learn new cognitive skills (new ways of thinking), seemed to offer a real chance of enabling these children, first, to recognise their inappropriate behaviour, and second, to challenge previously ineffective thinking patterns, so allowing them to make new choices about their (to them) confusing, and (to others) disruptive, behaviour.

Confidentiality

Intricate issues of confidentiality and law need to be addressed when working with children, especially in the context of schools. This chapter is not able to engage in a full discussion of these complexities. Briefly, however, I have found it essential to discuss boundaries at the beginning of assessment, making it clear to the children that any disclosed facts which indicate they are at risk from others or from themselves would mean that I would have to inform parents, GPs and/or social services.

I have been challenged many times about the potential conflict between protecting confidentiality and trust, and what is in the best interests of the child. Parental custody battles and sexual abuse cases have meant that four times in two years I have been subpoenaed to court, with my notes, and with only twelve to forty-eight hours' notice. When this happens, the interests of school, clinic, child and law all need to be kept in mind. However, always paramount in *my* mind, as I and the child I counsel begin our collaborative venture, is what is in the best interests of that child, and my goal is always his or her emotional well-being. This is not necessarily the same *primary* goal as the school's.

Theory in context

> Men are disturbed not by things but by the views they take of them.
>
> (Epictitus)

Although there are potential conflicts inherent in my role as a counsellor who works in – but is not part of – schools, the CBT approach fits well into the culture of schools, both in its theoretical underpinning and the structure of its therapeutic process. In terms of the latter, exploration, study, homework and learning new information and skills are all familiar to pupils, while the pattern of each session, with its setting of goals, researching of problems and experimenting with new ideas, is quickly recognised. Both teachers and parents also easily relate to the CBT model, as it reflects the modern trend of asking children to determine their own personal profiles and devise their own goals. The collaborative process of CBT is familiar too, since it is similar to the way in which even young infant schoolchildren are taught at mixed ability tables where cooperation is praised.

The fit between CBT theory and educational priority and practice is also clear. A school's primary task is to nurture children's cognitive abilities – their capacity to 'accommodate' new information: to learn. Accommodation is a fundamental cognitive concept (Piaget 1952) which describes the way in which the acquisition of new information leads to an adjustment to, or change of, an existing belief. Since our early beliefs, inevitably based as they are on limited views of the world, constantly need to be revised and updated, the process of accommodation promotes healthy adaptation and growth.

In contrast, 'assimilation' is the process by which new information is integrated into powerful pre-existing beliefs. Thus Sam, who believes that he is bad and unlovable, and that his parents penalise him whenever they ask him to do something, is only able to hear whatever supports these beliefs. So when his mum says, 'We *do* love you and, because we care about you and your well being, we want you to go to bed *now*', the information offered is assimilated wholesale into his pre-existing belief system – that he is bad and his parents are punishing him – without reference to his parents' actual tone of voice or facial expressions or to their declaration of love. In other words, Sam's learning is partial and his cognitions (his thinking) 'distorted'.

A child's cognitive processes then – be they clear or 'distorted' (Beck 1967) – are affected by their underlying 'assumptions' (Beck 1976) or beliefs – be they 'adaptive' or 'maladaptive' – about themselves, the world and their futures (Guidano and Liotti 1983).[2] It has been established, for example, through clinical trials and research, that clinically anxious children are more likely to expect bad things to happen and are less likely to anticipate good things. Thus they tend to assimilate rather than accommodate new situations, so strengthening their distorted beliefs.

These children evaluate themselves more negatively, with greater levels of negative thoughts about feared events and tasks (Kendall and Chansky 1995). Depressed children present with similar pessimistic thinking styles and have poor problem-solving skills – they too show 'cognitive errors', including 'catastrophising' and 'over-generalising' (Kaslow *et al.* 1994) (see below for an illustration of these terms). These errors inevitably affect all areas of their learning, both social and academic.

Clinical work

CBT focuses on the meaning a child gives to events, since it is this meaning that determines our behaviour. A primary task of CBT then is to uncover what these meanings might be, by teaching the client (child) to become aware of what Beck calls their 'automatic thoughts' – the thoughts and images occurring involuntarily in the 'stream of consciousness' (Beck 1967). If these are always distorted – for example, negative, or highly critical – learning is likely to be hampered and an emotional or behavioural disturbance may result.

Once the nature of the negative thinking has been uncovered, and the feelings and events that have triggered it identified, the counsellor helps the child to understand the connections to the emotional, behavioural or learning problems they may be experiencing. After this, a child's goals can be shaped according to desired outcomes; perhaps new feelings and behaviours which are wanted. Working together with the counsellor, the child's thoughts and beliefs are treated as hypotheses in scientific experiments, available for testing to discover whether they are true or false. Challenging any unrealistic or self-defeating thinking with contradictory evidence, the child is helped to create and support new, more functional ways of thinking.

Referring to the experimental nature of this cooperative counselling method, Beck *et al.* (1979) use the term 'collaborative empiricism'. Collaboration is key from the start, with counsellor *and* child participating in setting the agenda for each hour-long session. Homework is also an important element, used in part to reinforce new thinking skills and problem-solving techniques, but also to encourage practising the practical. Agreeing on the week's homework during the session enables the child to take some personal responsibility for the material covered, and so allows for the growth of self-confidence. It also facilitates the counselling to be more effective more quickly, and results in short-term work of, usually, eight to twelve sessions. In addition, CBT can usefully contribute to the personal and social education element of a school's curriculum, since it lends itself to being used in an instructive way. Indeed, some young people respond well to the reframing of counselling as coming for 'personal development', or to see a 'development coach'.

A note on assessment

A thorough assessment is crucial for gathering information about a young person's perceptions of their problems, the specific symptoms, the behaviour involved in the presenting problem, and the perceptions of the family and the school. It is only then that a suitable strategy-and-implementation plan can be devised to suit their particular needs. There are various clinically based questionnaires designed for children, which help the counsellor to measure the degree of depression or anxiety underlying seemingly unrelated behaviours. These make a significant contribution to creating a conceptualisation of the case or, in fact, can highlight whether there are indications that CBT counselling would be unhelpful.

> John, aged ten, was referred with behavioural problems by his school. His scores indicated no significant depression or anxiety but what soon became apparent was that there were many family difficulties, particularly concerning sibling rivalry. It was important not to collude with the school's and the family's belief that it was 'John who had the problem', and it was suggested that family therapy, rather than individual CBT counselling, was a more appropriate intervention.

CBT employs a Socratic questioning style which is empowering for teenagers, helping to mitigate the hint of coercion contained in some schools' suggestion that if they don't attend they may be suspended or excluded. Questions such as: 'Why do you think you are here?' 'How do you see yourself?' 'How do you think you fit into your surroundings?' allow the young person to be seen as the one with meaningful answers – especially important since, in such cases, a counsellor can meet a great deal of resistance in entering into the therapeutic relationship.

Case study: Jane

Assessment and formulation

Jane, aged sixteen, was referred by her school because she had become increasingly tearful in her lessons, saying she could not cope with the work. Although a bright girl, in the top sets for all her subjects, she had recently begun to fall behind. Her tutor was at a loss to know what the problem was. Jane attended the assessment alone, not wanting her parents to be involved, and made it clear at the outset that she had only come because her tutor suggested it. She herself was very unsure whether counselling would do her any good.

Jane cried throughout the assessment, saying that she was a failure at everything. Through her tears, a few facts emerged. She was the younger of two children in an intact nuclear family. She said she got on quite well with her family, who were all high achievers. Her brother Paul, aged seventeen, had excelled at everything, and she thought that no matter what she did she could not compare with him. Yet everyone expected her to be like him. Recently, however, the family had said they were sick of her moods and Jane herself was harshly self-critical, saying that she hated herself – that she was fat and useless.

Even when Jane achieved a B+ in an essay, she was unhappy because it was not an A. Having very high and somewhat unrealistic expectations of herself, she worried a great deal about her perceived sense of failure. Her scores on the Children's Depression Inventory indicated mild clinical depression, and also exhibited a lot of general anxiety about life. My initial thoughts were that her underlying problem was one of low self-worth.

Jane agreed to attend an initial six sessions, after which we would review how she thought things were going. I then explained the CBT approach to her, and, with specific information from our session, we used the following simple model of quantifying feelings.

JP: When you arrived at the beginning of our session Jane, can you recall you told me you were feeling very anxious, and when I asked how you would measure it on a scale of one to ten, you said 'nine'?

Jane: Yeah.

JP: Well, I'm wondering how you are feeling at the moment?

Jane: Yeah, I was feeling really anxious when I got here but I feel much better now.

JP: So how would you score your level of anxiety now?

Jane: I think about four out of ten.

JP: That's good, so it's reduced. Can you remember earlier we explored what you were thinking to make yourself anxious?

Jane: Yeah, I thought: 'What will the counsellor be like?' 'She might think I'm stupid.' 'She won't be able to help me.' 'She might not like me.'

JP: Right, and now I'm curious about what thoughts you have at the moment?

Jane: Well, I think you're OK, really. I feel a bit better talking about my worries. I'm glad I've come to see you now. It's been helpful.

JP: So, can you see your thoughts have changed since you came to the session, and that because you've changed your thoughts, your feelings have also changed and now you feel less anxious?

Jane: Yeah, I see what you mean.

By focusing on Jane's thoughts and feelings and measuring their intensity, Jane began to make connections about the relationships between them, and to understand the impact her 'thinking' was having on her feelings and behaviours. I asked Jane what she wanted to achieve from counselling and in her life generally. We agreed that goal identification/goal setting could be some useful homework which we could then discuss at our next session.

Course of treatment

Jane's 'automatic thoughts' were recorded in homework diaries and used to help make links between the thoughts and her subsequent actions. Our initial alliance was strengthened around a mutual attempt to find some relief from the internal pressure that Jane expressed as: 'It does my head in.' I also asked Jane to keep a daily mood chart, noting when she had felt sad, listless, unhappy, etc. We engaged in some simple role-play, where Jane was invited to imagine that her friend was sitting beside her: she had to advise the friend, who was having a bad day. Jane was encouraging with her 'friend' yet critical of herself – much more forgiving of other people than she was of herself – which she eventually began to see was unhelpful.

One analogy that seemed to help Jane was this: I asked her to think of her favourite car. If one of the tyres had a puncture, would she just junk the whole car? Certainly not! So why would she want to junk herself for getting a B+ rather than an A? Gradually, Jane began to think about being a friend to herself. Interestingly, on making a tentative list of her strengths and discussing this with her family and friends, Jane was surprised to find, and found it hard to believe, that they said many positive things about her. This did not fit with her underlying negative self-beliefs about being useless. This exercise helped Jane to see that her beliefs were not entirely accurate.

CBT focuses on clarifying any 'cognitive distortions' presented and helps to formulate ways to change them. As we persisted in checking out and challenging such thoughts as 'I'm useless', and 'I'll never be good enough', Jane realised that her thoughts *were* distorted and not really a true reflection of how things were. Together, we investigated the information-processing errors (see below) which resulted in her misconstruing a teacher's laugh. Jane said that a teacher had laughed at her, pointing out two spelling mistakes in an essay for which she had received a B+. She took this as evidence of her poor ability in essay writing. By confronting Jane with the following specific cognitive distortions (distorted thoughts) that had led to her misconstruings, she was able to begin to see that in fact there was little or no evidence to support her deeper negative beliefs.

SELECTIVE ABSTRACTION
Jane selected one aspect of a situation and interpreted the whole on the basis of the one detail. Jane said she thought her work was not good enough and that 'I keep making mistakes'.

ARBITRARY INFERENCE
Jane reached a conclusion without evidence. She said, 'He thinks I'm useless' despite having got a B+.

OVERGENERALISATION
'I can't do anything right.' 'No one appreciates how hard I try.'

MAGNIFICATION AND MINIMISING
'Fancy making two mistakes, I must be really stupid.'
'He probably just felt sorry for me, so he gave me a B+.'

MIND READING
'I know he doesn't like me.'

PERSONALISATION
'I know Mr Smith is stressed and it's probably all my fault.'

CATASTROPHISING
'I'm failing at maths. I'm going to fail at everything. What a disaster! I can't stand it!'

In addition, Jane agreed that she could ask her English teacher what he thought about her work. She was able to clarify that her original negative inference about the situation was incorrect, and that in fact the teacher thought highly of her, and her work.

It is of central importance to be clear about whether any strongly held belief is accurate, or erroneous and therefore unhelpful. We spent many sessions exploring Jane's 'assumptions' or 'underlying/core beliefs'.

Jane: Sometimes I'm in a bad mood and I don't know why – I just cry in my room.

JP: Is that all day?

Jane: Well it's mostly when I get home, after school.

JP: What do you think triggers your bad mood?

Jane: Well, I suppose, when I think about studying and the exams coming up.

JP: What are the thoughts that go through your mind at these times?

Jane: Well, I go home and I plan to do some revision and then I think I can't be bothered so I'll do it later.

JP: So then what happens next?

Jane: I end up thinking, 'I don't want to do this.' 'I don't feel like it.' 'I don't know where to start.'

JP: So when you have all these thoughts: 'I don't know where to start', 'I don't want to do this', 'I can't be bothered', what does this mean to you?

Jane: That I'm a failure and I'm useless and it's all a waste of time. I'll never achieve anything.

JP: And when you think that, how do you feel?

Jane: I feel down and miserable.

Jane thought about some positive, self-calming statements she could use when she felt anxious. This worked well for some issues, but not at all well for others. Different methods were then employed. One of Jane's more distressing images of herself was as a fat and ugly girl – and this despite presenting as a very slim and attractive one. To begin to understand how Jane's vision of herself operated, we drew a line representing a continuum of human shapes and sizes, with very fat on one side of the page and very thin on the other. I asked her to place herself where she thought she belonged. She put herself on the ninetieth percentile of fatness. We then looked at her image in a mirror, checked the size of her clothes, and examined a chart of height/weight ratios. All these supported the reality that she was well within the normal weight range for her height and age. She also placed Kate Moss, Dawn French, her mother and her friends on the continuum. Jane's perceptions were distinctly distorted and she began, slowly, to recognise this. After this discussion, and with a great deal of trepidation, she was able to place herself within the normal weight range, although she struggled to acknowledge this discovery and it took several reviews of the facts before she began to feel comfortable.

During these first six weeks Jane was better able to acknowledge that she *did* sometimes feel loved by her father, who had come to her room on several occasions, and had been quite emotional as he told her that he loved her for herself and just wanted her to be happy. She was also able to talk about her relationship with her mother, and her brother, of whom she felt quite jealous. Jane was noticeably more uplifted in her mood and was no longer tearful by the time of her review, and said that she believed counselling was proving helpful. She was thinking and feeling more positively about herself, although she still struggled with ideals of perfection and with low self-esteem.

One of the distorted cognitions that caused her most difficulty was that relating to outstanding scholastic success equalling personal success. The corollary was particularly true – imperfection equalled personal failure and subsequent rejection. When Jane looked for the origins of this belief, it emerged that her parents had separated for a short time when she was seven and, in her seven-year-old mind, Jane had concluded, 'It must be my fault. I was too naughty. I wasn't good enough.' So Jane thought there was something wrong with her and developed two implicit beliefs: that if she had been good enough, 'Dad wouldn't have left', and 'I have to be perfect or others will reject me'. Plucking up courage, Jane decided to talk to her mother about her memories of the earlier separation, and her mother was able to explain briefly that it was a difficult time, reassuring Jane that the marital difficulties were not in any way her fault. Jane expressed strong emotions during her sessions, which highlighted the intensity of her core beliefs, and she became angry with those around her: in particular with the teachers who had commented to her, on several occasions, how well her brother had done and said, 'If you could only do half as well, it would be great'.

In the final phase of treatment, we discussed letting go Jane's drive for perfection and how, in some ways, she wanted to be very much like her mother and brother. In this way, she came to see her punishing academic efforts as a way of trying to feel close to them. Gradually, Jane began going out and about more often. Her mood elevated further and stabilised, and she began to show a sense of humour about having driven herself so hard. She was also pleased she had achieved some good grades and caught up with her school work.

Conclusion

School league tables are now a fact of life and, in an increasingly success-driven culture, some schools are struggling to deal with their 'problem' children, just as those children struggle to cope with school and the pressures of contemporary life. If not helped, the danger is that they will fall further and further behind their peers, both socially and academically.

Finite resources need to deliver a counselling service, but are also expected to combat increasing drug and alcohol abuse among young people. The CBT approach offers a very effective way of working with young people, validated by research findings,[3] and has the added benefit of possessing a theoretical underpinning and a structured process in accord with the culture of schools. The process of accommodation, promoted by CBT techniques, finds a natural home in schools, where we expect our children to challenge beliefs and to reach out for new understandings. When children reach their full potential, both emotionally and educationally, this brings benefits not just for the child but also for the staff and the school community as a whole, an outcome which satisfies both me *and* the school.

Notes

1   All clinical material has been provided by June Platts. June Platts and Yuki Williamson have worked together for a child and family psychiatric service, using CB and psychodynamic approaches respectively.
2   Although CBT was originally devised for adults, it has been adapted for use with children and adolescents (see Braswell and Kendall 1988; Stark *et al.* 1991), and I myself have developed many strategies and techniques to suit differing age groups' needs. Often adults are not aware that young children and teenagers get depressed or suffer from anxiety problems, rather they perceive that a child is lazy or difficult. Frequently, children present with low self-esteem, masquerading as, among other things, poor academic performance, wildly disruptive behaviour, bullying, weepiness and angry outbursts.
3   Children as young as eight years old have benefited from CBT (Spence, Australia 1994). Research at a Birmingham child and family service has shown 87% of children recovering from depression following CBT (Feehan and Vostanis 1996; see also Harrington *et al.* 1998).

References

Beck, A. T. (1967) *Depression: Clinical, Experimental and Theoretical Aspects,* New York: Harper and Row.
—— (1976) *Cognitive Therapy and the Emotional Disorder,* New York: International Universities Press.
Beck, A. T., Rush, A. J., Shaw, B. F. and Emery, G. (1979) *Cognitive Therapy of Depression,* New York: Guilford Press.
Braswell, L. and Kendall, P. C. (1988) *Cognitive-behavioural Methods with Children,* New York: Guilford Press.

Feehan, C. and Vostanis, P. (1996) 'Cognitive-behavioural therapy for depressed children: children's and therapists' impressions', *BABCP Journal*, 24(2): 171–184.

Guidano, V. P. and Liotti, G. (1983) *Cognitive Processes and Emotional Disorders*, New York: Guilford Press.

Harrington, S., Whittaker, J., Shoebridge, B. and Campbell, S. B. (1998) 'Systematic review of efficacy of cognitive behavioural therapy in childhood and adult depressive disorder', *British Medical Journal*, Vol. 316, Department of Psychiatry, Royal Manchester.

Kaslow, N. J., Brown, R. T. C. and Mee, L. L. (1994) 'Cognitive and behavioural correlates of childhood depression', in W. M. Reynolds and J. F. Johnston, *Handbook of Depression in Children and Adolescents*, New York: Plenum Press.

Kendall, P. (ed.) (1991) *Child and Adolescent Therapy: Cognitive-behavioural Procedures*, New York: Guilford Press.

Kendall, P. and Chansky, T. E. (1995) 'Considering cognition in anxiety disordered use', *Journal of Anxiety Disorders*, 5: 167–185.

Piaget, J. (1952) *The Origin of Intelligence in the Child*, New York: International Universities Press.

Spence, S. H. (1994) 'Cognitive therapy with children and adolescents: from theory to practice', *Journal of Child Psychology and Psychiatry*, 35: 1191–1228.

Stark, K. D., Rouse, L.W. and Livingston, R. (1991) 'Treatment of depression during childhood and adolescence: cognitive-behavioural procedure for the individual and family', in P. C. Kendall (ed.), *Child and Adolescent Therapy: Cognitive-behavioral Procedures*, New York: Guilford Press.

Chapter 8

Using art and play in assessment and intervention for troubled children

Hilary Hickmore

Introduction

Part of the role of an educational psychologist (EP) is to provide assessment, consultancy and interventions to enable children (including those with emotional and behavioural difficulties) to access education. In contrast with most counsellors working in schools, they do not see children as a result of self-referral but when teachers and/or parents ask for their involvement. By this time, teachers, parents *and* children are often under a great deal of strain. Having already put in considerable time and energy to no avail, there is likely to be a sense of frustration, distress and hopelessness around the difficulty ever being resolved.

Before EP involvement, most teachers in primary and secondary school, mainstream and special, will have applied (perhaps unknowingly in some cases) behavioural principles in their assessment of, and intervention strategies with, children and young people showing emotional and behavioural difficulties. Substantial time is devoted to collecting data on antecedents, background factors and consequences of students' behaviour, so that patterns can be revealed and elements modified in order to effect behavioural change. Those who have taken on an additional cognitive element in their perspective discuss these patterns with the students concerned. They set targets with students and discuss how to achieve them. They agree celebrations on successful achievement of targets and monitor their progress in relation to them. The quality of the goal setting and review sessions engaged in can be such as to be worthy of the term 'counselling'. They are respectful conversations, aimed at improving the experience of the child in school, valuing what the child brings, listening to the child's perspective, accepting her view of the situation, and facilitating her in working out how to bring about change.

Cognitive and behavioural perspectives provide the predominant models underlying the work of many counties' behaviour support teams and support agencies when they are asked to assist in assessment and planning for children showing emotional and behavioural difficulties. Educational psychologists often combine traditional cognitive-behavioural approaches with cognitive therapies such as solution-focused therapy and personal construct therapy. They usually employ active listening skills derived from Rogerian counselling. In this way, they are able to bring something new to schools' work when their involvement is requested. They almost always take an interactionist perspective, being keen to observe the influence of the teaching, learning and peer environment of the child on her behaviour, rather than assuming that a problem lies 'within' a child. This draws EPs to observe a child in the classroom or in the playground, to look at teachers' behaviour, to explore the appropriateness of the curriculum and how the school policy is applied. EPs and their colleagues in child and adolescent mental health teams often apply systemic thinking and approaches in working with a child's family.

There are many examples I could offer, where combinations of these prevailing perspectives have been drawn together to assist teachers and parents in forming a coherent and effective individual education plan for a child. Sadly there are many examples where such plans, though coherent, have *not* been effective in bringing about significant change in children's distressing and challenging behaviour. Indeed, during my first two years as an EP, I became increasingly concerned at the lack of impact that carefully devised interventions were having. Being new to the profession and having naive faith in my psychological perspectives, I made the assumption that it was the way the plans were executed that was the problem. Exploring this hypothesis, however, I found I could not hold on to this belief. Excellent practice *was* going on, carried out by deeply committed teachers, special needs assistants and caring parents, yet still to no avail. What was worse, the children for whom my advice was not working were the ones whose behaviour was at the extreme end of the continuum. They were the ones for whom, when interventions did not bring about change, exclusion became the school's only option. It was the children who showed violent outbursts; who shouted abuse at teachers; who withdrew into themselves; who hid, rocked, engaged in obsessive behaviours; who damaged property, stole things or bullied relentlessly; whom staff did not understand and who did not understand themselves. They were the deeply unhappy ones, the ones who felt helpless, stuck and without hope.

My search was defined then as one which would offer something more effective for these children, their parents and their teachers. This chapter describes some key finds from that search, including:

- the importance of assisting children and young people in expressing their perspectives, feelings, understandings and needs using art and play;
- the therapeutic use of art and play in providing children of all ages with a way of exploring, examining and reconsidering the troubles they experience;
- the more comprehensive understandings to be gained by drawing on the principles of other key perspectives, namely Gestalt and transactional analysis (TA).

Theory

Facilitating communication using art and play

Children experience enormously complex mixes of feelings and views in relation to relationships and experiences. I have found that the visual creative product, arrived at through playing with toys, miniatures and art materials in the context of a counselling session, enables this jumbled, overwhelming mix to be disentangled, separated and then considered bit by bit in manageable chunks. As Cattanach (1994: 18) writes:

> as the child plays, she uses toys to represent her emotions and thoughts symbolically. It is this combination of cognitive sorting of experience and the personal emotional expression of experience which helps the child integrate and make some sense of what has been happening in her particular world.

What the child works with in play is not confined to the rational here-and-now, for play 'draws on fantasy and on the total reservoir of what might be dreamed, and of the deeper and even the deepest layers of the unconscious'. In the symbolic acitivity of play, 'one thing "stands for" another, and the consequence is that there is a great relief from the crude and awkward conflicts that belong to stark truth' (Winnicott 1984: 95).

It seems to me that this is the essence of what makes play and art helpful and *safe* in counselling children who show emotional and behavioural difficulties. Every child I have come across, who has shown behaviour difficulties in school and has not been able to verbalise valid reasons for her behaviour, has had some troublesome issue she is facing (or has faced) and is trying to manage it. Perhaps it cannot be talked about because, being too painful to contemplate, it is kept out of awareness, or perhaps it reflects so monstrously on her family as to be seen as disloyal to reveal it. When working with symbols, however, all these dreadful meanings can be brought out and used experimentally and in dialogue with the counsellor because the child is *not* asked to use the currency of 'stark' reality or 'truth'. As Liebmann (1986) suggests, in this way children can re-enact problems and conflicts 'in safety, without fear of real consequences' and 'perhaps by changing the outcome . . . become more able to deal with the problem in real life' (p. 13). Both Storr (1972) and Gersie and King (1990) comment that there is a need to distance oneself from a profound emotional experience if one is to contemplate and reflect upon it. Symbolic expression in art and play facilitates this distancing.

I use art in a number of ways. First and foremost, I use it as an extension of non-directive therapeutic play. Children and adolescents can play spontaneously with various art materials and act out a story or make a scene that is important to them symbolically, just as they might enact one in role-play or with toys or miniatures. Art is enormously useful in both directive and non-directive work, having the added advantage that children are able to keep the 'product', return to it, think about it again, add or change things. When children are willing to be directed, creative activities can be posed which relate directly to key emotional and behavioural themes that have been reported. Furthermore, where appropriate and in accordance with the children's wishes, their art products can be shared with key adults who need to understand their issues more fully. Showing parents what children have made can have much more of an impact on them than a second-hand reported account of something they have said. I will discuss such sharing of information with others in more detail later.

Drawing on TA and Gestalt principles

It is not enough simply to use art and play to assist children in expressing their emotional world. This work needs to be done within a theoretical framework. The framework gives the work its direction and coherence. It provides the EP/counsellor with a language for explaining what the child has done, and how it relates to her behaviour. It enables the consistency and constancy that derives from working to a sound set of principles.

Creative activity is used within a number of psychological orientations and philosophies. In my work, I draw primarily on key principles and concepts derived from Gestalt and transactional analysis (TA). I have found that these theories complement the predominant perspectives in use in education and are immediately accessible to teachers, parents and older children. With new understanding about behaviour, teachers and parents often relate differently (and more helpfully) to a child. Change in their interaction with the child is more fundamental and enduring when it stems from a shift in their understanding. With new understanding, a child may be able to let go of negative assumptions about herself, such as being mad, not likeable, a weirdo or rubbish, and start to contemplate a new self-concept.

It is not the key focus of this chapter to give a detailed exposition of Gestalt or TA perspectives in counselling. However, I shall highlight some of their principles, where they have proved particularly useful in promoting understanding and new ways forward for children who show persistent emotional and behavioural difficulties.

Gestalt and TA are both firmly rooted in humanistic philosophy. There is a fundamental assumption that children will strive towards growth. The task of the EP/counsellor is to facilitate their self-awareness and expression of thoughts, feelings, beliefs and perceptions. With this new awareness, change will then naturally follow as the child accommodates this new understanding, takes up her own will to apply it in the world to her best advantage and lets go of old, immature perspectives and patterns. Humanistic approaches place the client in the responsible position of knowing what she needs. It follows then that it is the *child's* understanding of her world, and *her* meaning in any symbolic representation of it, that the EP/counsellor works with and that teachers and parents are asked to consider in planning interventions. Pertinent here is Maslow's view of a good therapist as one who helps his client 'to unfold, to break through the defences against his own self-knowledge, to recover himself and to get to know himself' (Maslow 1971: 50).

Fritz Perls, the founder of Gestalt psychotherapy, trained in psychoanalysis; hence there are many aspects of psychoanalysis embedded in Gestalt thinking. A key assumption, for example, is that much of children's behaviour has its source in understandings and feelings of which the child is not consciously aware. These understandings and their related emotions were rational and necessary at the time they were first experienced (taking into account the child's developmental level), but the behaviour unconsciously arising from them may seem irrational and unexplainable in the present (see Clarkson 1989). The relief on the part of teachers, parents and older children is immense when the essential logic of an intense emotional outburst or persistent behaviour difficulty is revealed. There may be no logical explanation in the here-and-now setting in which the behaviour takes place, but when past meaning is taken into account, satisfying explanation is almost always attainable.

Alice had been leaving classrooms in the middle of lessons several times a day for her entire school career. Now twelve years old, she had been excluded from one school, yet was continuing this behaviour despite a clear target to stay in class, sanctions for leaving, close monitoring and regular reviews involving her and her mother. No logical triggers or benefits had been identified. Having been asked to carry out a new assessment to shed some light on this persistent behaviour, a priority task which followed from embracing the principle described above was to take a full family history from Alice's mother. She revealed that between the ages of one and eight years old, Alice had been repeatedly locked in her bedroom for several hours at a time during her fortnightly visits to her father. It would be inappropriate to reveal any more detail here. Suffice it to say that a new hypothesis about Alice's absconding emerged, and it was seen much more in terms of her needing to escape from a classroom in which she felt increasingly imprisoned. This was stirring the powerful feelings of desperation and abandonment that she had frequently had to push out of awareness for many years. As well as arranging counselling, I was able, with the mother's agreement in sharing this information, to help Alice's teachers take an entirely different approach to encouraging her to stay in lessons.

Another key Gestalt principle is the notion of *the whole being*. People are said to have four parallel domains which make up their whole being: body, thought, emotion and behaviour (Clarkson 1989). These are inextricably bound together. A response in any one of the domains will have a parallel response in all the others. If we wish to tune into what a child is wishing to express and assist her in exploring it further, we need to listen to and reflect back not only thoughts and feelings, but to notice and work with *the way* she says what she says and makes what she makes. Gestalt counsellors 'go with where the energy is'. This means looking for clues in the child's body and movements about areas of tension or activity, focusing on them, exaggerating them and using them to enable the expression of the same issue in the other domains (Oaklander 1988). This principle is clearly illustrated in the work I describe with John later in this chapter.

Perls was strongly influenced by Gestalt psychology, a theory of perception being explored in Germany in the 1930s and 1940s. The natural tendency to create a meaningful whole out of an incomplete image was used by Perls in relation to all human understanding and emotion, not just sensory perception (Perls *et al*. 1951/1969). He suggested that children, in the absence of all the necessary information around a troubling event in their lives, will make up the missing items, so that it becomes meaningful and complete. This 'inappropriate closure' means they can carry with them some false and unhelpful understandings which affect their behaviour for many years. When we consider John's story, we will see how counselling helped address the inappropriate closure he had made.

TA was developed by Berne in the 1950s and 1960s. It provides a detailed technology for exploring and understanding what is going on in the often puzzling interchanges between people. Two concepts I find particularly useful are 'personal scripts' and 'rackets'.

Everyone is said to have a life script, laid down in the first few years of life, largely through the experience we have of the world. This underpins our developing view of who we are, our relationship with those around us, and what we can expect out of life. For example, once a child has 'decided' that the world is a terrible place which will hurt her and in which she will never have her needs met without pain, she will relate to the world from this set of assumptions. She will seek to confirm these assumptions and, due to the subtle way in which unspoken expectations tend to become reality, will generally achieve that confirmation. Where the child receives contrary messages, these will be rejected or in some way destroyed. This transaction is known as a 'racket' (Berne 1961). For example, the child whose script tells her that no matter how hard she tries she will always disappoint others, on receiving genuine praise for school work well done, will seem hugely uncomfortable and subsequently do something that will attract disapproval. The task in counselling is to uncover and explore these 'life plans' as an 'aid to making changes' (Lapworth *et al*. 1993: 101).

Clinical work: using art and play in schools

In my work as an EP, I use art and play in two ways:

1   as a means of assisting children in communicating their perspective during assessment;
2   as a method in counselling that I undertake directly with children.

Assessment

The most immediately exciting and satisfying application of art and play in the school setting is seen in the assessment process. In assessment, all involved are seeking to clarify the main factors affecting the child and her behaviour, and to determine how to make changes to influence her behaviour. When the predominant approaches have been used; when parents have been fully involved; when teachers demonstrate good class-room management skills and have placed emphasis on valuing the child and building a positive relationship; when useful data have been collected and discussed and acted upon; when despite all of these things the resulting intervention has not worked, it is time for the tick charts, monitoring forms and target sheets to be laid to one side. These usual assessment tools are replaced by crayons, enormous sheets of coloured paper, clay, a box of pipe-cleaners, building blocks and play people.

When using creative expression in assessment, the whole emphasis is on finding out about the child's experience and communicating findings to those who need to know. No counselling contract is entered into. No confidentiality agreement is made. I explain the context very carefully to the child, so that she knows that this is to gain some understanding of the muddles and troubles that may be bubbling away inside, with the aim of teachers and parents knowing how best to help her feel better. When able to be directed, I ask children, for example, to choose a piece of coloured paper that is like the horrid feelings they sometimes have inside; to draw something on the paper that seems to make the horrid feelings happen; to imagine their perfect day and draw it or make it in some way; to put stones on to a page to represent themselves and all the important people in their lives, in positions that feel right; to make something that shows what their classroom is like. When they are too frozen by their need to hold on and survive, I just open up my cases of materials and toys and enter into a non-directive style. Whatever is made becomes the subject of further conversation, the EP/counsellor making non-judgemental comments, reflecting back, clarifying and 'promoting the child's further self discovery by asking her to elaborate on the parts of the picture' (Oaklander 1988: 53). In so doing, the child reveals important information about the way she is experiencing her world and what the key issues are for her, that were previously unavailable for expression in words. She may reveal some of her life script or an inappropriately closed Gestalt. Once revealed, as well as the child seeing new ways forward, adults are enabled to see practical changes they can make that were not obvious from evidence gathered previously.

Amy, aged six, was a well-groomed, alert and polite little girl, who appeared rather tense and jumpy. She had been refusing to go into her classroom, becoming abusive and violent if staff tried to force her. She had also recently become unwilling to let her mother leave her after bringing her to school in the mornings. She could offer no spoken explanation for her behaviour. School staff were at the end of their tether. They did not have the resources to supervise her for the lengthy periods of time she was spending out of the classroom. Reluctantly, they were considering exclusion.

Assessment preceding my involvement had revealed difficulties with writing and spelling skills, about which she was sensitive. An individualised literacy programme had been set up to address this. She had been set targets about going into class in time for registration and allowing her mother to leave, and her parents had agreed to follow up on certain rewards on achieving weekly targets. Nevertheless, the situation was deteriorating.

It soon became apparent when I met Amy that we would not gain anything by talking about her school and home experience. Everything was rosy, in words. When I asked her to *draw* her classroom however, she chose red paper for 'angry feelings'. She drew a boy breaking her model and a girl (the child she had been asked to sit next to) hitting her, and blood spurting out of the wound. She went on to say how this girl teased her about her writing, not loudly and obviously, but in quick, quiet comments and in her tone of voice and negative looks. When I asked her to make something to show the feelings she had when she was refusing to let her mother leave in the morning, she made a soldier out of play dough. The soldier was attacked by snakes, shot at by other soldiers and drowned on a raft. Amy's father was in the army. I asked her how she felt about this. She replied that every day she was 'frightened to death in the heart' that he would not come home because he would be killed.

Clear, actionable plans came out of this assessment information:

* for Amy's father to take her to his office and show her how safe his job was in reality;
* for the class teacher to change seating arrangements in class;
* for the teacher to tackle teasing and 'put-downs' as part of her class' personal and social education programme.

These strategies, together with being given a security-inducing reception into class each day and an incentive to be in class by a certain time (for that would mean she could undertake a special job for the teacher), led to success. Full attendance in lessons was achieved within two weeks and sustained for two terms of follow-up. My challenge here was to be flexible in applying different theories and related techniques. This meant I could assist Amy in expressing her perceptions about her world using one set of approaches, then switch modes to propose cognitive and behavioural interventions that staff and parents could undertake. This is the strength of being an integrative practitioner.

Clinical counselling as part of a multi-faceted individual education plan

Counselling using art and play may feature as a clearly defined element of a multi-faceted individual education plan for a student. This is the work of trained and supervised counsellors and therapists, and has optimal potential for bringing about change (within an affordable time scale) when these personnel work collaboratively with parents and school staff. EPs who offer counselling are in a particularly helpful position, since their relationship with schools is already one in which it is expected that they will join teachers and parents in joint problem solving, planning and review. It is expected that they will be interested in looking at all factors that are contributing to a difficulty. Having such a role means that any counselling they offer becomes embedded more easily within recognised special needs structures, takes account of local resource issues, is acknowledged as an intervention at Stage 3 of The Code of Practice, and becomes part of the child's individual education plan (IEP). The child's progress through counselling becomes as much a natural part of a review as her progress in relation to targets on her IEP and the impact of environmental changes and new teaching strategies. Changes and responses in school and at home can be noted, and inform the next IEP and the direction of counselling sessions. Conversely, key information and revelations made in the counselling sessions can, when the child allows them to be shared, inform planning and bring about huge shifts in stuck attitudes or negative patterns.

It is not usual to offer counselling without a firm and solid commitment to confidentiality (within child protection constraints) and I would not consider reducing the safety of the counselling session, in this respect, for children who have taken a great deal of time in being able to share anything of themselves. It is the case, however, that in using art and play, children can very quickly achieve new insights about themselves and their lives, and often very much want to share these insights. This is not just at the request of young children. Recently, for example, I spoke to Jonathan, aged thirteen, about the possibility of my contributing some information to his family group conference. I gave him the option of my making no contribution and maintaining confidentiality, or agreeing with him what, of the understandings we had reached about his extremely destructive outbursts, I could describe at the meeting. On the notion of confidentiality he said, 'What's the point in that? What is the point in you spending all this time if you never tell anybody?'

Counselling, using play and art, may be appropriate to include in an intervention where there are significant and persistent behavioural difficulties which are hindering a child's positive experience of education, and:

- her behaviour has not changed as a result of good teaching, and interventions by staff and carers focusing on her behavioural and thinking domains;
- she has been unable to engage with a cognitive-behavioural counselling approach;
- an assessment session reveals that the child is very defended about her feelings and certain aspects of her life, yet shows an interest in meeting again to do more;
- a single assessment session does not reveal enough to provide new insight on which to plan further aspects of an intervention to be carried out by school staff and carers;
- in the assessment session, the child enters into the activities fully and either reports or seems to gain significant release, relief or assistance from it;
- the child is distant, cut off, hard to build a relationship with, responds unpredictably and out of proportion to any stimulus, seems troubled and/or intense, yet in assessment can be engaged in aspects of the counselling process using play and creative approaches.

When offering play and arts counselling as part of the intervention for students, it is *their* agenda that is followed, at *their* pace. Hence this approach does not fit easily with six-week time-limited contracts or a particular brief (such as anger management) requested by teaching staff. Some students may feel they have learned some powerful new things about themselves after four or five sessions, and may need some space and time before undertaking further counselling, if indeed they do return. Others may need significantly longer. Some students will work so symbolically that the EP/counsellor may wonder if there is anything meaningful or purposeful happening at all, yet be surprised by teachers stating how helpful the sessions are, since Tony is 'so much more open and relaxed'. When the counselling session is experienced as meaningful by the child, she treats it seriously and respectfully.

John

I was asked to assist staff in a pupil referral unit (PRU) in planning the way forward for John, a bright, fifteen-year-old boy. When alone with an adult, John worked well on activities of his choice, but, once in a group, he seemed tense, defensive and angry. He appeared to spark off arguments, whereupon he regularly stormed out of the room and left the premises. He was also seen as being very resistant to adult instruction or request, and presented his carers with particular difficulty in this respect. My initial involvement included assisting staff in being more specific in their targets for him, discussing a tighter reward system, and passing on materials on anger management. The work set was appropriate and the general environment was positive, with an emphasis on valuing the individual and building relationships.

On review a month later, I found that staff had attempted the plan we had agreed, but that John had been very resistant to talking about the patterns of his outbursts, and had not been able to work towards the agreed targets about sitting down at the start of lessons and avoiding provoking the other students. The level of disruption to lessons and the amount of time he spent out of them had meant that an individual tuition programme had been set up for him. His mother, uncle and aunt had been involved in the decision making. No one knew why he was being so provocative and storming out. When asked, John just shrugged his shoulders; he did not know. John wished it was not so; he saw himself as out of his own control and thought despairingly about what the future held for him. He wondered if he was going mad.

John reluctantly agreed to meet me. He was fearful about what I would uncover about him. He was worried that it would be overwhelming. I assured him we could stop at any time, and that we would communicate using pictures and diagrams so that he did not have to put his feelings into words.

John sketched his life as a road, drawing with great care six hospitals which all looked exactly the same. He said these represented where he was born and all the important people who had died, as well as his pet dog. The most important of these was the first one to die, his father. He was then freed up to speak of how the intense pain of that and all the other deaths were with him *every* day. He talked of feeling so full of emotion that he felt he might burst into tears at any moment. The prospect of making such a fool of himself was too much to contemplate, so he avoided social situations. He particularly liked walking in the fields around his uncle's house. He could relax there. The only way he felt he could prevent the other students at the PRU from seeing how vulnerable he was was to attack them. He could not stay and cope with the ensuing conflict however, so he left the room.

I asked John if I could share with his family and teachers what he had drawn and told me. He agreed, but made it very clear that no other students must be nearby and able to overhear. I agreed to meet staff after all the students had gone home, and to speak to his family on the phone.

John's perspective gave all involved much more to go on. Individual tuition was seen not as an unfortunate arrangement because a plan had failed but as a key way of providing for John's education, given the emotional stress he was under. He was no longer seen as lacking in social skills, but as needing to withdraw socially while he worked through his grieving process. Counselling from CRUSE (a charitable organisation offering free counselling to those who have suffered a bereavement) was added to his intervention plan as one of the components. Sadly, at that time, my diary did not permit me to offer counselling directly. His carers realised the need to talk with him openly and honestly about his father's death.

John was unable to face meeting a new counsellor, and refused several appointments. After some months, I was able to set up a series of counselling sessions with him. After only three sessions, John started to reflect on his anger with the adults in his life and his refusal to listen to them. It seemed likely that his anger was rooted in conclusions he had made six years previously. This was when his father had died of cancer. No one had told the nine-year-old John that his father was dying. Perhaps they did not know how to. Perhaps they could not face it. Perhaps they felt they had to 'protect' him from the truth. Was it that his father could not bear him to know, or wished to deny to himself that he was dying as his way of coping? All John perceived at the time was that no one had been trustworthy enough to tell him the most important piece of information that he could ever need. This was John's 'inappropriate closure' to his confusion and lack of understanding.

John described how, had he known that his father was dying, he would have told him important things, and he knew his father would have had important messages to give him in return. He concluded that adults could not be trusted; they tell you lies. In TA terms, this became his personal script about his life and the adults in it. 'Adults will let me down; they tell me lies.' An angry disrespect for adults' viewpoints stayed with him from then on. However, once nine-year-old John's conclusions had been revealed, he realised there were other conclusions which fifteen-year-old John could make about adults. His disrespect, disregard and hostility faded and he completed his second work experience placement successfully, despite the fact that it required cooperative working with others. (The first one had been terminated two weeks early because of his refusal to listen to his supervisor.) His family reported how much more relaxed and at ease he seemed. At the end of the year John, his tutor, his family and I all agreed that he was in a position to look forward to a successful college placement.

John became able to express all these things so quickly by my following his lead. I trusted his direction, matched or exaggerated his energy and used my own creativity to suggest and develop activities that facilitated his symbolic and physical expression. Although he generally presented as very lethargic and low in energy, it soon became apparent by the second session that he needed to leap about and shout. To provide a forum for doing this in the counselling sessions, he chose the two soft balls I had in my case and we started throwing and bouncing them around the room. After a little of this, he constructed a mini-tennis court out of sheets of marked paper stuck on to a table top and added a pipe-cleaner for a net. We played with this for the second half of the session, improving our skills and fine tuning the rules. In the third session, he set up the soft ball mini-tennis game immediately on arrival. We started another vigorous game, and it was in walloping the ball with all the force and aggression he could muster that there was a suitable physical match for the power and aggression that was caught up with the feelings and thoughts surrounding his father's death. He spat out the words as he walloped the ball. He shouted, swore and cried as he told his story, seeming to highlight the most poignant parts with another slamming attack on the ball as he hit it back to me again and again.

It may be that John was so ready to explore the issues driving his behaviour that any form of counselling would have worked for him at the time. It seemed, however, that there was something enormously important in using his energy and letting our work be led by the very strong physical messages he was giving. Gestalt draws the counsellor to notice what the body is doing and to work creatively with any form of expression the client seems able to use at any one time. John felt he had done his work after this third session. He wanted to start getting on with his life with his new insights and increased potential to be who he wanted to be. He thanked me and declined any further appointments.

Conclusion

The principles and approaches described in this chapter are enormously valuable in understanding, assessing and assisting many children whose behaviour is not easily explainable by reference to obvious current factors. Irrational, impulsive acts, relentless bullying, over-activity, refusals, destructive acts, hiding, controlling behaviour, obsessive behaviour, stealing, hoarding and self-harm can be seen as in some way logical or helpful when we set them in the context of the child's past experience and life outside school. By exploring the influences of the past on the present and of elsewhere on the school setting, we open our assessment process and resulting interventions to a much wider and more comprehensive set of factors which influence behaviour.

The predominant cognitive-behavioural perspectives will always have a very central place in assessing and addressing the needs of children in schools. For some children, however, being able to express themselves using creative modes adds that something extra to free up stuck, hopeless, puzzling situations and enables them and the adults working with them to understand what is going on and hold some hope for the resulting way forward. When play and arts counselling is delivered as part of a multi-faceted individual education plan, in which clear roles, purposes and actions are specified for teacher, parent, classroom assistant, EP/counsellor and child working together, we have a much more powerful and holistic intervention which I have found considerably more effective in enabling a student (and key adults in her life) to let go of unhelpful patterns and move on to a more healthy and happy way of being.

References

Berne, E. (1961) *Transactional Analysis in Psychotherapy*, New York: Grove Press.
Cattanach, A. (1994) *Play Therapy – Where the Sky Meets the Underworld*, London: Jessica Kingsley.
Clarkson, P. (1989) *Gestalt Counselling in Action*, London: Sage Publications.
Gersie, A. and King, N. (1990) *Storymaking in Education and Therapy*, London: Jessica Kingsley.

Lapworth, P., Sills, C. and Fish, S. (1993) *Transactional Analysis Counselling*, Oxford: Winslow Press.

Liebmann, M. (1986) *Art Therapy for Groups*, London: Routledge.

Maslow, A. H. (1971) *The Farther Reaches of Human Nature*, Arkana: Penguin Books.

Oaklander, V. (1988) *Windows to our Children*, New York: Gestalt Journal Press.

Perls, F. S., Hefferline, R. F. and Goodman, P. (1951/1969) *Gestalt Therapy: Excitement and Growth in the Human Personality*, New York: Julian Press.

Storr, A. (1972) *The Dynamics of Creation*, Harmondsworth: Penguin Books.

Winnicott, D. W. (1984) *Deprivation and Delinquency*, London: Routledge, 1994.

Chapter 9

Promoting emotional literacy

Anger management groups

Peter Sharp and Elizabeth Herrick

Introduction

Several years of over-emphasis on the importance of cognitive development, and particularly the measurement of intelligence (IQ), seemed to us a significant mistake. The affective domain was at best being overlooked in schools, and at worst relegated to badly taught and undervalued personal and social education. When Southampton Psychology Service was created in April 1997, we were determined to incorporate therapeutic intervention as part of the work of all educational psychologists (EPs) in the team (currently fourteen EPs) and to utilise a variety of psychological models. So it was then that we decided to try and work towards restoring the curriculum balance, by promoting 'emotional literacy' in Southampton schools.

Our belief that emotional intelligence is at least as important as cognitive intelligence was triggered by the work of Howard Gardner (1993) and reinforced by the work of Daniel Goleman (1995, 1998). The negative connotations associated with the term 'intelligence' led us to adopt the term 'emotional literacy'. This work was developed in parallel with the national literacy strategy, and seemed like a positive way to reframe or re-brand some older ideas. Steiner and Perry (1997) argue that emotional literacy is made up of three abilities: the ability to understand your emotions, the ability to listen to others and empathise with their emotions, and the ability to express emotions productively. They further assert that to be emotionally literate is to be able to handle emotions in a way that both improves personal power and the quality of life around you.

Emotional literacy is now a published priority in Southampton's strategic education plan, alongside literacy and numeracy as an equal partner. Southampton defines emotional literacy as helping people to develop 'the ability to recognise, understand, handle, and appropriately express their emotions'. Our published hypothesis is that if pupils are emotionally literate, which includes feeling positive about themselves, they will learn more effectively. We have a city-wide aim of establishing emotional literacy at the heart of the curriculum. Improving anger management for teachers, parents and children is one important part of this process and another published priority.

Teachers were telling us that there seemed to be an increase in the frequency and severity of challenging behaviour, and that they felt ill-equipped to manage this despite overhauling their behaviour policies and trying to 'catch children being good'. This basic behaviour management technique works well with most children, but for those with very challenging behaviour, something more was needed. So it was then that we began, in 1995, to develop a training programme for children, parents, school staff and governors about *anger management*.

Since most angry children are particularly poor at managing their own behaviour in group settings, paradoxically, we chose to adopt a group approach. There *are* economic and time constraints which mitigate against extensive individual work, particularly when it is our aim to promote this work in virtually all schools in Southampton. However, the rationale for our work is driven largely by therapeutic considerations, as we firmly believe that more can be achieved in groups and more rapidly too. The opportunity for young people to practice, *in vivo*, positive anger management and other social skills, and to be regularly and publicly reinforced for their efforts, is the main reason why a group approach is more likely to be successful than individual therapy or counselling.

Together with our colleague, Adrian Faupel from Southampton University, we quickly realised that what was needed was a more direct form of intervention, and the first *anger management group* was established. It was run over six sessions with six pupils identified as being at risk of exclusion as a consequence of their challenging behaviour and, more particularly, their poorly developed anger management skills.

The first two groups were run in mainstream primary schools in Southampton, each with two educational psychologists and two teacher observers. The results were sufficiently encouraging, both in terms of the outcomes for children and the systemic shift in schools mediated by the teacher observers, that we refined the model. Subsequently, we tried it in a mainstream secondary school and then in a secondary school for children with emotional and behavioural difficulties, and still remained optimistic that it had real value for children and teachers. In addition, we began running training courses on anger management for teachers and learning support assistants, and workshops for parents. At the time of writing, we have run forty-five anger management groups in thirty-eight schools.

Working in the context of a local education authority means that we have a number of stakeholders with a legitimate interest in our work. These include the LEA, the schools, the parents and the children, and our colleagues in other agencies. The challenge for us has been to accommodate the needs of all our stakeholders while providing therapeutic interventions for our children and young people which make a difference in a timely and effective way.

Theory

> We choose to view anger as a *secondary emotion* that may arise from a primary emotion such as fear. Fear may be bound up with embarrassment, disappointment, injury, exploitation, envy, or loss. All of these feelings represent a *threat* of some kind, albeit that we often don't recognize this while angry. If anger becomes significantly disruptive in a child's life, this may lead to emotional illiteracy. This is likely to persist through adulthood unless support is offered and accepted.
>
> (Faupel *et al.* 1998)

In addition, we consider anger to be a *reflection of emotional difficulties* which may lead to, or arise from, emotional disorder. For children, the roots of such disorder are often known to teachers, parents and carers, but they receive a planned and sophisticated response less frequently. Furthermore, we hold that anger is an *instrumental behaviour*, which achieves particular outcomes and may be part of what some writers describe as conduct disorder. It can be seen as attention-seeking behaviour, or perhaps is better described as attention-needing behaviour, since the anger is expressed usually as a result of a lack of positive attention in a child's formative years.

Anger is an essential part of being human, has evolutionary or adaptive significance, and is either useful and positive or harmful and negative. At first reading, this may appear an untenable stance, but we hold that anger is a paradoxical emotion. Many, if not most people think of anger as largely or wholly negative, but we label that as *problem anger*. Useful anger is that expression of feeling and thought which asserts our right to have our needs met without violating the best interests of others.

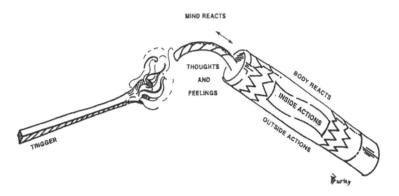

Figure 2 The Firework Model
Source: Adapted from Novaco's model for Anger Arousal in Feindler and
Ecton 1986

Our work makes extensive use of the Firework Model (Figure 2), as
children and adults readily understand it. The *trigger* is likened to the
match that ignites a *fuse*. The *fuse* represents the mind reacting and the
thoughts and feelings a person has. The *firework* or *explosive cylinder*
represents the body responding physiologically and may lead to a
destructive explosion of anger.

We also use the metaphor of *the storm*, to help children (and adults)
understand the bigger picture and the role of environmental influences. In
practical terms this may enable us to help children learn to read the signs
of a storm brewing and so use some (taught) strategies to head off expressions of problem anger. Failing that, it may help them to weather some
storms more effectively, and especially without hurting others. We also
encourage youngsters to learn from even the most distressing examples of
problem anger, rather than suppress or deny its significance.

These then are the metaphors or models we use to explain how anger
works and so offer children a way of 'recognising' and 'understanding' this
emotion. Novaco (1975, 1978), describing some of his own clinical work
– using the Firework Model – as 'self-instructional training' identifies
what is essentially a cognitive-behavioural approach. Indeed, the very fact
that we *teach* the model fits well the pedagogic nature of the traditional
cognitive-behavioural method. However, it is an eclectic theoretical base
which informs both the way we run the groups and our subsequent analysis
of what has occurred.

Cognitive approaches

Emphasising the difficulties that can occur when the nature of thinking adversely affects behaviour, we challenge the children when they show what Aaron Beck (1988) calls 'cognitive distortions' or 'distorted thinking' (see Chapter 7). For example, we try to surface the internal dialogue ('automatic thoughts') when they are angry, or are recalling times or events when they *were* angry, so that we can invite them to question and test its (their) validity.

Beck describes how cognitive distortions and their underlying 'maladaptive assumptions' – the rigid and unrealistic rules which an individual uses to interpret events and so guide behaviour – can lead to inappropriate outbursts of anger (1976). Again, we use this concept to help children examine their 'maladaptive assumptions' and move towards more helpful and positive thinking.

In a related way, we may also help children to consider what Albert Ellis (1994) calls 'irrational beliefs' which, like 'maladaptive assumptions', are absolutist, dogmatic and tend to lead to inflexible behaviour such as 'problem anger'. We then offer alternative views and beliefs by considering the different potential outcomes.

Behavioural approaches

Some members of the groups we have run have found it very difficult to cope with simply being in a group. We try to use high frequency 'reinforcement' ratios to encourage them. The use of reinforcement to modify behaviour is a key technique in behaviour therapy (Skinner 1974). Its use is based on the principle that if a consequence is provided for a certain behaviour, that behaviour will become strongly associated with it. In effect, the consequence becomes a reinforcement. Thus 'positive reinforcement' is where the behaviour is strengthened by the contingent presentation of a 'reward', while 'negative reinforcement' is where the behaviour is weakened – made less likely or even 'extinguished' – by the contingent presentation of a 'punishment'.

Contemporary behaviour therapy tends to emphasise the efficacy of positive reinforcements (see Spiegler and Guevremont 1993). In our groups, we deliberately use very frequent positive verbal reinforcement together with more tangible rewards (stickers, certificates, refreshments) and try to avoid negative reinforcement by frequent reinforcement of the established ground rules. The strongest negative reinforcement we have used is temporary removal from the group, which has only happened on a handful of occasions during forty-five groups. It is also worth noting that children who are 'on report' within the school system are often very keen for the psychologist to complete the report at the end of the session, as psychologists are less reserved in their praise!

Some of the games we use in the sessions even employ the use of a 'token economy'[1] whereby participants are rewarded for effort or positive comments by receiving tokens, and the winner for the day is the child with the most tokens. It is astonishing to see how simple rewards can be so motivating. Yet many of the children we see are simply unused to receiving immediate and regular reinforcement for successive approximations to desired goals or behaviours.

Social learning approaches

Albert Bandura (1969) originated the view that social behaviour is effectively learned through seeing how others behave in particular circumstances. Essentially, this means that if 'problem anger' has been learned, new, more effective ways of dealing with anger can also be learned (1973). This can, in part, be achieved by 'modelling' appropriate behaviour for the child to imitate. This is a view which is particularly helpful in encouraging teachers to be more optimistic about a child's capacity to change, despite a long history of acting-out, challenging behaviour. It is also a concept which group leaders can put to good use within the anger management group.

Psychodynamic approaches

Our belief in the effectiveness of the group setting is strong. However, some children need to be supported in their development with individual work, either instead of or in addition to the group. Where this is so, a more psychodynamic approach may help the child to gain deeper insight into the 'why' question in relation to their problem anger. Almost without exception, such children have had difficulty forming secure attachments (see Chapter 6) in their early years, or have experienced the kind of disruption to such attachments that John Bowlby (1973) has described as reducing self-esteem.

Finally, we tend to employ a psychodynamic perspective among ourselves, reflecting on the dynamics of the group process both in the debrief after the session and at subsequent whole team supervision.

Whatever theoretical base we use, however, we aim to help children to explore, and so better manage their:

- thinking
- feeling
- behaviour.

Clinical work

Establishing a positive context

Working with staff and parents: creating supporting structures

Prior to running a group, we have a planning meeting with key staff in every school, and introduce both the theory and practice involved in making a group run successfully. This includes explaining the roles of the adults in each group: the psychologist who acts as *group leader*, and two teachers whose roles are those of *co-worker* and *non-participant observer*.

The co-worker needs to be an experienced and senior teacher who is motivated, enthusiastic, and able to work well with small groups of challenging youngsters. He or she intervenes as little as possible in the running of the group, but as often as necessary – for example, to help students with reading worksheets or cards. It has been richly rewarding to work with some very talented and capable teachers in this role, but we have had some real difficulties with a few teachers who simply cannot distance themselves from a didactic authority role, despite encouragement and explanation. Nevertheless, we are committed to this collaborative approach as our aim is to embed such work in the culture of schools and to empower teachers to work in more creative ways with some of the most vulnerable youngsters in school.

The observer also needs to be an experienced and senior teacher. Observers take notes on process and content, as they see it, and they often contribute useful insights in the debrief at the end of each session. They also act as 'escort' if a student has to leave the group.

In addition, we also aim to have a *mentor* for each group member (e.g. form tutor or class teacher) who meets with the child briefly on a daily basis to give support and encouragement and to take responsibility for making sure each child does the homework set at each group meeting.

We offer in-service training to all school staff, and increasingly parents too, on *Anger Management*.[2] This training is essential if teachers and parents are to support the programme and consider their own anger management. We also aim to provide opportunities for parents and staff to work together on issues, since providing combined and consistent support from both home and school is particularly effective in helping children and young people make sustained changes in their behaviour.

Training for interested staff is also important, as it can, after several groups have been run, help to promote systemic shifts in schools. Further, staff involved in running the groups commit to providing support for other staff as and when it becomes appropriate. The school liaison psychologist also provides ongoing support via regular meetings.

As for the psychologists working as group leaders, weekly supervision is available. Currently, this is provided in a group in order that support and ideas can be generated in the interaction with others doing the same work. Individual supervision is offered if the work becomes particularly challenging, or if the group leader concerned feels a personal need for one-to-one support.

Working with students: establishing the frame in which work is done

Currently, schools choose the students to be involved and then obtain informed consent from parents. Students have largely been drawn from a cohort of those 'at risk' of permanent exclusion, many of whom have already been excluded from school for a fixed period or have exhibited some very challenging behaviour. Nevertheless, a student's own sense of *responsibility* and *motivation* are essential preconditions for successful outcome. Thus after parental permission has been granted, each potential group member is seen, prior to the beginning of the sessions, in order to explain what will happen within the group and to ensure that the young person feels able to ask questions and make a personal decision about joining the group. If the young person decides to join, some work is then done to provide a baseline for the pupil's own perception of their difficulties, in order to begin the process of empowering them to take responsibility for their own actions.

Explicit *ground rules* also need to be established in order to promote the likelihood of success. First, participants should attend on a voluntary basis. If they choose to leave, then they return to lessons, or if their behaviour is really poor, we construe this as their decision to leave the group. Second, participants and group workers should aim to be positive. Third, no one should intentionally do anything to hurt or upset another group member (so no name calling, 'wicked looks', negative comments or put-downs). Finally, we assert that we learn best by taking turns and listening, so interruptions are discouraged and taking turns praised. These ground rules are printed and given to participants as laminated cards (the size of a credit card) and rehearsed at the start of each session, essentially as a way of creating clear boundaries for us to work within.

The *venue* is the responsibility of the school. It should be fit for the purpose, free from interruption, and preferably remain the same for the duration of the group. Refreshments – a drink and a biscuit, for example – are provided at the end of each session, and *not* on a contingent reward basis. More accurately, participants receive the reward as long as they remain in the group. While this may seem trivial, we believe that such rewards may well be the most tangible symbols of nurturance that some children ever experience receiving in school.

In terms of *timing*, the sessions last fifty minutes, with students, having had refreshments, leaving as the hour ends. At this point, the group leader (the psychologist) and the co-worker and observer (the teachers) have a short debrief led by the former – what worked well, improvement suggestions, issues arising, troubleshooting and so on. The timing issue matters because schools run on 'bells'. Children need to go where they are expected or it can cause problems for both receiving teachers and late-arriving children.

Finally, the participants all have a *manual* or *learning log* and schools need to have spares. Most students seem relaxed about paying a nominal sum for replacement, and it encourages them to take responsibility for their property.

Groupwork: content and structure

Session 1: Introduction

In this session we use appropriate games aimed at developing rapport, exploring strong feelings in a safe setting and increasing awareness that we all have very powerful feelings. Homework is to keep a diary focused on noticing what goes well in school that week.

Session 2: What makes me angry

Having reviewed the diary, we consider the question 'What is anger?' This is a brainstorm activity, and we try to get everyone involved. Next, we pose the question 'What makes me angry?', using a published worksheet we have developed. Next, the Firework Model is introduced and each of the three components are discussed. We have also used a three-dimensional model to great effect, especially with children aged between five and fourteen. Homework is to log any time when you get angry, saying what happened, how you felt, and how it ended (Firework Model, Figure 2).

Session 3: The Anger Solution Game

Reviewing the homework 'What makes me angry?', we explore the variety and nature of triggers. We then play the Anger Solution Game (Shapiro *et al*. 1995), a board game which explores alternative ways to handle anger and aggression. Homework is to interview someone in your life whose self-control you admire.

Session 4: Face It

Again, homework is reviewed in an attempt to extract any important learning points. Next, we complete a worksheet entitled: 'How do I feel?' Then we go on to play 'Face It' (Shapiro *et al*. 1995), a card-game which helps children to 'read' facial expressions and provides an opportunity to comment on the feelings these portray. Homework is a worksheet entitled 'Anger management – keeping calm'.

Session 5: Defence and threats . . . puppets

After reviewing the 'Keeping calm' homework, each participant chooses the name of an animal from a list and then writes a short script to show (1) what the animal does when it is threatened (defence); (2) how the animal threatens others; (3) what the consequences of 'your' animal's behaviour are (e.g. a bee dies if it stings). Each participant is given a puppet of 'their' animal (none of them know this is coming) and are asked to introduce 'their' animal using the script they have just written. Homework is about learning how to use 'I messages' instead of 'You messages'.

Session 6: The future . . . ways to manage

This is a video-based, anti-bullying session (e.g. *Sticks and Stones* – Carlton Television), introduced by asking participants to define and discuss bullying before using the video to stimulate further work on how to reduce or prevent bullying. As part of our managed ending, we discuss the 'Daily Personal Peace Plan' (Shaprio *et al*. 1995) and hand over to school staff to carry on the work we have done.[3]

Certificates and stickers are awarded to participants and teachers. We laminate ours and hear that they're treasured by some students! At the end, we aim to have debrief interviews with staff and pupils.

Groupwork: intervention, process and change

We have now worked with well over two hundred and seventy children and over eighty adults during the forty-five groups completed, but the following description attempts to capture just some of the flavour of what we do by using brief vignettes.

In all counselling work, we are trying to help the client to bridge the gap between wanting to change and the reality of responding in known and practised ways when outside the counselling context. Within six sessions of groupwork, we aim to give back the responsibility for behaviour to the young person, and to support them in working towards getting angry less frequently and in a more controlled and less destructive way. Support for this, within the school and home context, has been described above.

The young people chosen for our groups are those who have no explicit repertoire of positive strategies to choose from when they face difficulties, their current responses to triggers being routinely negative and antisocial. Within the group setting, a safe environment is provided in which young people can explore their belief systems and discuss alternative behaviours, then try out new strategies that are provided.

The importance of voluntary participation became clear early in our work. One participant in a group of six boys, aged thirteen years, became very disruptive in the group, teasing and name calling and interfering with the group process to the point of stopping the session. This was a young person who had been moved between foster placements on numerous occasions and was currently undergoing another change in his living arrangements. On discussion with the young person, it became clear that he felt he was not being treated with respect by adults generally and had very few choices in his life. Attending the group was interpreted as another example of losing control in his life and being 'pushed around' by adults. Discussing the voluntary nature of the group with him and his ability to make choices within it enabled him to feel positive about rejoining the group and participating effectively.

Within another group, the importance of the initial meetings became apparent when one of the pupils made it clear that he could not attend the group, as his brother was going to be in it as well. In discussion with family and school, it became clear that it was a combination that was unlikely to enable either of the boys to feel able to discuss their feelings openly.

Alternative arrangements were made for supporting one of the boys. The importance of valuing young people's perspectives cannot be under-estimated in the context of running emotionally safe and effective groups.

It is important that the group leader helps the young people to adhere to the ground rules in order to keep the group physically and emotionally safe. To do this, he or she will use adult and peer reinforcement, as well as encouraging the young people to reflect on how their actions might be affecting others in the group. Direct reinforcement is provided by noticing and rewarding desired behaviours – e.g. taking turns, listening without interrupting, waiting for attention – and ignoring other behaviours where appropriate and safe – e.g. leaning back on chairs, pen tapping, looking out of the window.

Whole group reinforcement may be appropriate in some instances. For example, a group of fourteen-year-old girls, all of whom had significant emotional and behavioural difficulties, and some of whom had learning difficulties, found it particularly difficult to concentrate, take turns and not to tease and make remarks in response to each others' comments. Placing counters in a cup whenever good behaviour was observed helped members of the group to consider the consequences of their behaviour in a tangible way. Clearly it was important to negotiate the reward prior to the session, and in this case the girls had particularly enjoyed the game that had been played in the first session and had asked to play it again on several subsequent occasions. In this instance it was appropriate and relevant, therefore, to use an extra ten minutes with the game as a reward for making good choices in their behaviour.

With more able groups, it has not been necessary to make rewards as tangible and extrinsic as in the above example. The importance of peer approval is often effective as a reward for appropriate behaviours. One participant in a group was naturally impatient and found it difficult not to answer questions for the rest of the group. There was also a boy in the group who responded particularly slowly (he had a physical disability). Having been interrupted on several occasions, he was asked how he felt about other people answering his questions for him. He was able to tell the group, in an appropriately assertive way, that he found it annoying. A discussion ensued about whether our perceptions of being helpful were always accurate, and this was then related to other examples in the school and home setting. Using young people's behaviours to help them reflect on the effect they may be having on others helps them to increase their understanding of social interactions and how alternative perspectives can lead to misunderstandings, anger and even fights. Being able to discuss behaviours in a non-pejorative way, in an environment which is being kept safe by adults, is a major factor effecting change within the groups. The added reward of achieving peer approval by making small changes in behaviour is a very powerful reinforcer in groups. Within the example given above, both pupils had an opportunity to 'reframe' the others' behaviour in a positive way. First, the interrupting behaviour could be perceived as an attempt to be helpful, and second, the response that it was 'annoying' could be seen as assertive and positive. Staff later said that these two boys had previously got into difficulties in the playground as they 'wind each other up'. It is easy to see how both of those behaviours could quickly escalate into a battle if there was no understanding of each other's perspectives.

It is often difficult for parents to feel supportive of the work being done in the groups, especially if it has not been discussed with them directly. A fourteen-year-old girl refused to complete any work in her booklet after the second session. It was some time before the discovery was made that she had taken the picture of 'anger' home, which she had completed in the session. It had been torn up, as it was not considered to be of a 'good enough standard' for her. In contrast, a parent, who had her own fears about anger in the family, was able, after being given considerable time to express these fears, to support each session actively.

Recognising the importance of such interactions which occur in the broader context in which groups are run and giving them due time and attention has become an important part of our learning. Again, this was the case with one father whose particular concern was that we might be encouraging children to 'get it all out' within the group. He was worried that his son would be encouraged to display 'explosive anger' in the group. This cathartic method is not one which we adopt. For this father then, it was important to know how the group worked as well as what it was for.

The psychodynamic notion of containment (see chapters 1, 5 and 11) is also important for the group leader and co-worker to keep in mind. It is important that young people feel they can express strong feelings and that adults will be able to 'hold' them, not be damaged by them, and enable them to feel good about themselves afterwards. Children who have difficulty expressing their emotions appropriately have often been given the message that it is too dangerous to express how you feel, as you will hurt, upset or challenge the adult in an unacceptable way. Unfortunately, strong feelings may then 'leak out' when they are not expecting it, some-times with the wrong person and often in an uncontrolled way which violates the rights of others. One of the strong messages within the work we do is that we all have the right to have feelings and to express them, but not at the cost of someone else's right to be safe. It is important to get our own needs met but not by violating others. As such, the importance of containing strong feelings for pupils, while they begin to explore how they can express them more effectively, is a vital role for the adults in the group.

Within a group of ten-year-old boys, two of whom were particularly volatile, a fight broke out within the group setting. It was quickly stopped by the adults and the two boys were given time to calm. While calming, the rest of the group discussed how we could support them when they came back to the group. Both boys felt able to return and, within the safety of the group, were able to listen to advice and support while expressing their own views about what had happened. This resulted in spontaneous apologies from both boys and helped them to determine strategies that they would try to employ another time. It was important that the young people were not made to feel guilty, as this leads to lowering of self-esteem and a higher probability that situations will be interpreted negatively in the future. Understanding their own part in what had happened and making plans for future action were important. The young people could see that their strong feelings had not destroyed the group, neither had it destroyed their relationship with the group. They did, however, receive powerful messages that a more appropriate way of dealing with their feelings was necessary.

Reflections of the purpose of particular behaviours is used within the groups to help young people become aware of their behaviours and make choices about whether or not to continue with them. For example, in one group, one of the participants chose to tear at the corners of the paper of his booklet throughout the session. By pointing out that this behaviour might suggest a level of anxiety, it was possible to highlight the behaviour in a non-pejorative way and offer an interpretation of how it could be seen by others to reflect an emotional state. The young person was then in a position to choose whether or not he wished to be viewed in this way and to choose his behaviour accordingly. In this particular instance the behaviour stopped, though the pupil needed some support to maintain its cessation. Furthermore, attention given in this way to an individual also raised awareness of general anxiety within the group, giving all the members an opportunity to be supportive of each other and establish a more comfortable feeling within the group.

The role of nurturing within the group has been directly addressed by providing refreshments at the end of each session. The relationship between trust, positive behaviours and nurturing was directly observed in the group of thirteen- to fourteen-year-old girls with emotional, behavioural and learning difficulties. Over the six sessions, a fascinating shift in their behaviour within the refreshment period was observed. In the first instance, the arrival of drinks and biscuits instigated a rush to 'take' as much as they could within the time available. Gradually, however, they became able to wait, 'give' to others, negotiate and tolerate individual differences. As their emotional needs were being met through nurture, trust and positive regard, they were more able to respond to others' needs in the group. Although it might be argued that a novelty factor could explain the shift in behaviour, a commonality across groups, showing direct correlation between emotional need and the importance of nurturing, irrespective of novelty, supports our interpretation in this instance.

The variety of responses by staff within schools to the giving of refreshments has been interesting in itself. The contrast has been between those who have enjoyed providing quality choices with an air of celebration at the end of each session and those who, despite advice and discussion prior to the work, have felt unable to serve refreshments if they feel that pupils have not 'deserved' them. The learning point for us has been that it is genuinely too difficult for some staff to accept that young people, who are perceived as being badly behaved, can be supported by providing a therapeutic and nurturing environment. This is perceived as inappropriate reward for children who do not 'deserve' it.

Conclusion

The examples given above demonstrate the theoretical base that has guided our work, while highlighting the elements within the process that we consider to provide optimum conditions for change. We believe that a successful group is one in which the young people develop at least one or two new strategies to try in difficult situations, as well as having a conceptual framework with which to understand their own and others' anger.

Successes for us have included the following changes for young people:

* being less at risk of exclusion from school – fewer aggressive outbursts
* taking more responsibility for their own behaviours
* making connections – 'ah-ha' moments within the group work as well as some fundamental changes within the broader environment
* shifting staff perspectives on working with the young people
* working with parents to provide a consistent and supportive approach.

Evaluation has been on both quantitative and qualitative levels. Rating scales filled in from the child, teacher and parent perspective have been used before and after, with some evidence of perceptions of change for some children. Harder data have also been collected in terms of fixed term exclusions, and major incidents in school. We are now developing methods of bench-marking behaviour (e.g. incidents, detentions, letters home, etc.) before the groups are run, after they are completed and some time later. To date, the indications are that the groups do make a difference and that it is more marked for particular individuals, as would be expected. Structured interviews are also used with the pupils to gain some understanding of their perception of change. Almost all students who have participated report that they have enjoyed the group and most have said that they would recommend it to friends.

There is a need to make our evaluation tighter, and we are working on a clinical audit model in order to provide more consistent data over time. Specifically constructed questionnaires for staff, parents and children will be devised as well as establishing a baseline of behavioural incidents in school. A review of the first forty groups run in Southampton shows that the key determinants of success include: commitment of school staff to the process, the voluntary nature of participation by children and young people, adhering to the programme but tailoring it to the literacy and cognitive level of the group, and parental encouragement for children's participation. As our experience grows, we are becoming clearer about what works well and how to provide the optimum conditions for the development of emotional literacy. Anger management groups have an important role to play in making this happen.

Acknowledgements

We would like to thank Adrian Faupel for his massive contribution to our earlier work. We only wish we could spend more time on shared projects. Many warm thanks to the talented and enthusiastic educational psychologists in Southampton who have gone the extra mile in making these groups really successful across the city. Our appreciation also goes to senior education officers and (head) teachers in Southampton whose commitment and enthusiasm to making this work happen is heart-warming. It is beginning to help one of the least loved and lovable group of students we know. To the students we say . . . may your anger be forever well managed!

A final word of thanks from Peter to Lindsey, Chloe and Poppy and from Liz to Rick . . . well done for putting up with us!

Notes

1 For an evaluative review of this conditioning method, see Kazdin and Bootzin (1972).

2 This training has been evaluated very highly by over twenty-five audiences comprising a total of over four hundred people.

3 A summary of our *Model for Running an Anger Management Group* includes detailed planning with key staff in schools and parents, using a checklist which we describe as 'Steps to Success'. We can be contacted at the following address for further details: Southampton Psychology Service, Frobisher House, Nelson Gate, Southampton SO15 1GX; e-mail: p.sharp@southampton.gov.uk

References

Bandura, A. (1969) *Principles of Behavior Modification*, New York: Holt, Rinehart & Winston.

—— (1973) *Aggression: A Social Learning Analysis*, Englewood Cliffs, NJ: Prentice Hall.

Beck, A. T. (1976) *Cognitive Therapy and the Emotional Disorders*, New York: International Universities Press.

—— (1988) *Love is Never Enough*, New York: Harper & Row.

Bowlby, J. (1973) *Attachment and Loss, Separation: Anxiety and Anger*, Harmondsworth: Penguin Books, 1975.

Ellis, A. (1994) *Reason and Emotion in Psychotherapy* (2nd edn), New York: Birch Lane Press.

Faupel, A., Herrick, E. and Sharp, P. M. (1998) *Anger Management – A Practical Guide*, London: David Fulton.

Feindler, E. L. and Ecton, R. B. (1986) *Adolescent Anger Control, Cognitive Behavioural Techniques*, New York: Pergamon Press.

Gardner, H. (1993) *Multiple Intelligences: The Theory in Practice*, New York: Basic Books.

Goleman, D. (1995) *Emotional Intelligence*, London: Bloomsbury Publishing.

—— (1998) *Working With Emotional Intelligence*, London: Bloomsbury Publishing.

Kazdin, A. E. and Bootzin, R. R. (1972) 'The token economy: an evaluative review', *Journal of Applied Behavior Analysis*, 5: 343–372.

Novaco, R. (1975) *Anger Control: The Development and Evaluation of an Experimental Treatment*, Lexington, MA: D. C. Heath.

—— (1978) *Anger Control: Cognitive Behavioural Intervention*, ed. T. J. Forey and Rathien, New York: Plenum Press.

Shapiro, L., Shore, N. M., Bloemker, G., Kahler, D. S. and Schroeder, J. M. (1995) *The Anger Control Survival*, Pennsylvania, PA: The Center for Applied Psychology.

Skinner, B. F. (1974) *About Behaviorism*, New York: Knopf.

Spiegler, M. D. and Guevremont, D. C. (1993) *Contemporary Behavioral Therapy* (2nd edn), Pacific Grove, CA: Brooks/Cole.
Steiner, C. M. and Perry, P. (1997) *Achieving Emotional Literacy: A Personal Program to Increase Your Emotional Intelligence*, New York: Avon Books.

Chapter 10

Working with stories in groups

Gill Morton

Introduction

Most children come to school with a 'space' in their minds ready for new ideas. However, some arrive with that space already occupied – with worries about the safety or health of family members, by questions that cannot be asked or that no one has answered, by muddle about an inappropriate role in the family. Because such unprocessed pain is brought to school – a world with rules, authority figures and expectations about learning – being curious, making links and thinking with others can seem too challenging. School tasks can then feel 'toxic' and, activating painful issues and dilemmas, can become a 'brick wall' for both teacher and child. The result: hopelessness, passivity, disruptive or cut-off behaviour.

Children who have had to be vigilant for domestic or political violence will not easily pay attention to the book on their desk or their teacher's voice. A child from a critical home may doubt ever getting things right. Competition for adult attention or negative judgements about behaviour and achievements can reinforce parental messages about some perceived flaw in the child, and criticism can feel more painful than a teacher might think.

There is a parallel between these difficulties experienced by children and those experienced by adults in school (Salzberger-Wittenberg *et al.* 1983). Children *and* teachers can hate feeling that the world is out of their control and can struggle with criticism when being assessed. Both may feel unsupported, unheard, uncontained, overwhelmed and unable to think. This chapter describes groupwork with troubled children and their teachers using story-telling. Utilising principles and approaches of educational therapy, it considers some of the emotional difficulties of teaching and learning and describes some of the opportunities arising from this form of therapeutic groupwork.

Theory

Educational therapy

Educational therapy is a way of working with children whose learning and school behaviour are affected by emotional and social factors (Caspari 1986). It is a highly contextualised, specialist form of clinical counselling, since it not only focuses on the child's capacity to learn but also uses structured educational activities 'so that the therapist is able to observe both the child's reactions to formal learning situations and the defences the child uses to deal with anxiety' (Dover-Councell 1997: 12).

Problems with school tasks can be a sign of underlying difficulties, yet the curriculum *can* provide a new thinking space and an opportunity for issues to be worked through. For this reason, educational therapy also seeks to promote 'therapeutic opportunities' within the life of the school: times when teachers can pay thoughtful attention to difficulties and make creative use of opportunities within the curriculum to promote a safe space for thinking. This is easier when teachers can think about the impact on themselves of children's communications in which they may act as 'a receiver/focus for feelings that the child puts into [them], often ones that "belong" to earlier relationships or that the child himself cannot stand' (Dyke 1987: 52).

Drawing on psychoanalysis

Two psychoanalytic concepts are drawn upon in this understanding of the child's emotional use of a teacher – *transference* and *containment*. Transference (Freud 1912) refers to the idea that new people and situations are experienced through the lens of the already known (see Chapter 4). Containment (Bion 1962, 1967) refers to the process by which an infant's confused and anxious communications are received, digested and returned in a form that makes sense. Through this process, the growth of thinking is encouraged (see chapters 1, 5 and 11).

Educational therapy also draws on related concepts of *attachment* and *the holding environment*. Attachment refers to the way an individual is linked emotionally with another person and is based on early interactional patterns with care givers (Bowlby 1988; see Chapter 6). Secure attachments provide children with an inner sense of security which enables them to explore more confidently. Insecure attachments undermine this capacity and can have a deleterious impact on school behaviour and achievement (Barrett and Trevitt 1991). In a related way, a holding environment

(Winnicott 1960), which describes the conditions in which an infant feels well held both physically and emotionally (see Chapter 2), promotes the capacity to be curious and creative, just as the lack of it inhibits this capacity (Winnicott 1971a: 86). Educational therapy emphasises the importance of all these concepts as a way of understanding blocks in learning, of linking children's difficulties in learning with teachers' difficulties in teaching, and of making best use of the 'therapeutic opportunities' available in the everyday life of the school.

Drawing on family therapy

In addition, educational therapy draws on ideas from family therapy, including:

- *Context.* Attention to context (family relationships, rules and events) aids understanding, while the use of context – for example, the resources of the family – increases the effectiveness of efforts to change (Dawson and MacHugh 1994).
- *Reframing.* By offering 'a new definition of the same circumstances', children and adults can be helped to get out of a 'negative circle' (Watzlawick *et al.* 1974).
- *Externalising the problem.* This approach 'encourages persons to objectify and, at times, to personify the problems that they experience as oppressive' (White 1988/9).

Clinical work

Therapeutic administration

Aims

Therapeutic groupwork offers children a weekly space for some 'containment' and 'digestion' of unmanageable feelings in the safe space of the curriculum over a period of six to twenty-four weeks. The 'metaphor' in story-making offers them space for expressing preoccupations while allowing adults to pay attention to undigested experiences and habits of thinking and behaving formed as a consequence, without being intrusive. It also offers children an experience of adults who can think together without certainty and disagree at times without conflict. In addition, it aims to contribute to and further develop teachers' observation and reflection skills in relation to vulnerable children and to increase their therapeutic repertoires by involving them in the selection and running of the groups.

Selection

At a meeting with staff, we make links between emotional factors and learning, and think about children who trouble them. Staff are asked to suggest children for therapeutic help, naming behaviours causing concern.[1] Resisting urgency to concentrate on the most disruptive pupils, we encourage thinking about the whole range of children who get stuck and trouble teachers. We try to move beyond the 'noise' of the disruptive pupils to hear also about silent, inhibited children who are not learning. In this way, we create a balanced group (gender, age, ethnicity, type of difficulty) of six children who demonstrate difficulties with tasks and /or relationships in school. One teacher is asked to work as co-worker with the group.

Structure and setting

The group takes place, uninterrupted, for an hour a week in the same room in order to offer a setting in which children feel emotionally 'held'. Time is set aside for preparation, post-group discussion between therapist and co-worker and discussion with other staff. Activities (warm-ups, story-making and 'choosing time') allow for noticing and naming difficulties while leaving children with their necessary defences.

The children are collected from class by the co-workers. The group room has a table, two large chairs and six smaller ones – important markers of expectations about group tasks and hierarchy. There are paper, pencils, colours, glue, scissors and folders, as well as a store of play materials and story-books.

Group leaders' tasks

The group leaders need to address four key tasks. They must:

- convey that things are different in the group from the classroom without undermining the school system;
- offer an experience of reliability while posing questions and naming difficulties rather than giving answers;
- create a sense of connectedness in the group while at the same time giving a child's individuality a place;
- offer a space for thinking about the unthinkable.

To illustrate how we addressed these tasks I use a number of examples drawn largely from the following groups:

- Group A: Andy, Annie, Alice, Angus, Amy, Alvin.
- Group B: Byron, Bruce, Barry, Beverly, Bina, Benton.
- Group C: Callum, Charlie, Chris, Colin.
- Group D: Denny, Doug, Dora, Darren, Dot, Angus (previously in Group A).

The work

Warm-up

Introductions are made with a beanbag which is thrown between group members. Members give their own name and ask the name of the person catching the bag. Children may voice questions about why they are in the group. Ideas about being bad or stupid are listened to and 'reframed' as everyone having different things that get difficult in class or playground. Children are told that we will be making stories and drawings together, and it is made clear that that these will be kept safe and not shown to other children.

Activities offering structure and choice follow, allowing the adults to demonstrate their capacity to notice, play and not always have all the answers. A child can 'pass' in these games but needs to stay at the group table and listen. We notice a difficulty in joining in, but give a child permission to keep his or her thoughts private.

One activity is a group version of the 'Squiggle game' (Winnicott 1971b). One person shuts their eyes and draws a 'squiggle' on a page. They ask the next person to turn the squiggle into a picture. Guessing highlights the possibility of different ideas and 'no right answer'. If a child feels too inhibited to draw, they 'pass' the squiggle on to the next person. When a picture is completed and shown, a new squiggle is made.

Another activity is a 'reminds me of' word association chain game. A word is written on a piece of paper and passed around the table. Each person can add a word to connect to the previous one. Ideas are stressed as more important than spelling or handwriting, and children are encouraged to 'challenge' if they don't understand a connection.

Even at this stage, one can see some of the life-views which colour a child's perceptions of school. Andy was 'greedy' for attention and at first found it hard to listen to others. He showed concern that our games were 'using up too much paper' in a world where all the trees were getting 'killed off by pollution', and anyway, he was sure the adults threw away all the children's work at the end of a session as we 'thought it was rubbish'.

Story-making: the group metaphor

A story theme contains an idea of a journey undertaken by the group members. It mirrors the life of the group with a beginning, middle and end and, like a real journey, it has possibilities of working together or pulling apart. The adults scribe the story, incorporating everyone's ideas and putting in some of their own. Children choose a colour for their words in the first session which stays constant for the life of the group. Some children remember everyone's colour from the start. Some remember their own but no one else's. Occasionally, children choose one colour but say at the next session that they hate it. Amy chose brown in her first group. In the following session she rejected it. It was 'a rubbish colour, a dirty colour' and she hated it. She wanted pink. Or 'pinky brown'. Of mixed race, Amy's mother had remarried and the new partner was white. Later, the teacher and I thought about this as reflecting a preoccupation with family life which could make sense of her 'off-task' behaviour.

Each week a new chapter for the journey is begun such as 'Getting started', 'Taking with us and leaving behind', 'Dangers ahead', 'A new place', 'The mystery box', 'Falling out' and 'Getting back'.

GETTING STARTED

The children are asked to draw themselves for a group picture. In a 'sea journey', a large boat is drawn on which members place their self-portraits. We observe how each child manages this task – tiny stick figures or huge bodies overfilling the page; smiling images, angry looking teeth, or sad down-turned mouths overwritten with an exaggerated smile. Mistakes that children don't quite obliterate can indicate a muddle, a wish not to think about something or a need to show a negative feeling inhibited by fear of a bad response. Children may feel that only smiles are acceptable and that negative feelings will incur punishment or rejection.

Some want a ruler, others a rubber. Some start in a rush. Seven-year-old Bruce, a noisy, boisterous boy, rapidly drew himself as a flying Superman. The only boy in his family, he was both indulged and made anxious by this role. Others cannot start, saying, 'I can't draw', or continually restart, saying, 'It's rubbish!' Alice kept starting to make a mark on her paper but seemed to get stuck. She said she didn't need help but asked for a rubber and kept her paper covered with her arms or her face covered with her hands. Anxious and withdrawn, she had hardly been to school between the ages of five and seven. She had found it hard to be away from her mother, who told us, 'Alice would even sit outside the bathroom door waiting when I went to the toilet.' Watching Alice struggling with her self-portrait was uncomfortable for the teacher in the group. In contrast, I was more in touch with Angus, who spoke volubly and movingly about his attempts to stay out of trouble in school and who seemed eager to participate. Later, in our post-group discussion, I felt optimistic. My colleague didn't. We explored how we had each been in touch with a different aspect of the group, epitomised by Alice and Angus, and how we needed to put these aspects together to make sense of the whole.

TAKING WITH US AND LEAVING BEHIND

A journey not only raises issues of how to get started on something new, but also how to leave something or someone behind.

Group members are asked to draw three items to take on the journey. This can indicate a range of wishes or fears about joining in. Some want to take their families as if unable to think of managing away from home, while others protect themselves in other ways from the pain of missing someone. One worried-looking girl brought a phone to stay in touch with her parents, and her cat for company. Another wanted to bring everyone. We suggested she draw 'photos' as reminders instead. Some bring things to share on the journey, such as a fishing-rod or a tent. Others bring items to keep themselves entertained in an isolated way, such as a computer game or walkman. Children may bring weapons to prepare for expected dangers and some, like Bruce, bring a Superman outfit as they are sure to be needed as rescuers. Some seem anxious about food for the journey and draw giant plates of chips or tuna sandwiches.

As the story develops, an anxious need to continuously ask questions prevents some from taking in any useful information. Some participate verbally but avoid putting anything on paper in case they get it wrong or show too much. Others get stuck in painful silence for the same reason. And all the while, we develop the metaphors at the heart of story-making as a space to explore the issues underlying these 'behaviours'.

DANGERS AHEAD

'Oh what can I see over there?' starts the next 'chapter'. In a boat story, 'something' was spotted under the water. The children made guesses as to its identity which were written into the story and formed the basis of more drawings.

In Group C, Charlie thought it might be a dead body. An anxious boy with two mentally ill parents, he had had suicidal thoughts. Having chosen yellow for his story words, he drew, in pale pink, an almost invisible body. Colin surprised us by putting the danger inside rather than under the boat, deciding there was a predator on board. Callum was sure that it was the wreck of the Titanic – likely to damage our boat and cause it to sink. We discussed how big we thought this boat might be, what we might do about the danger and why there might be a body in the water.

In Group B, Barry said there was 'a man needing help' as 'a swordfish is trying to catch him'. Superman Bruce offered to rescue the man saying, "'I'm the hero." All the fishes are saying "help" and the whale is beating up the shark – the octopus is saying "Oooh!"' Bruce's friend Benton, who we knew had very quarrelsome parents, drew two large creatures fighting beneath the boat, endangering its stability. Byron drew a whale under his boat and Beverly drew an octopus with a very human face and a whale. She said, 'The man is in the water. He can't swim. He is shouting "Help!"'. No one is helping him. The octopus and whale are fighting . . . it might squeeze the whale like a hug.'

Children can communicate a powerful sense of danger and a lack of an expectation of help. Beverly put herself in danger by falling off the boat and countered efforts to rescue her, saying, 'The shark came and said, "I'm going to eat you." Byron is putting the fishing line down to pull me up but it is not pulling me up.' One child drew himself shooting the shark, but Beverly insisted that he had missed it and shot her instead.

Experiencing Beverly's pessimism led to a useful discussion. In both class and group she was 'off-task', interrupting or clinging. The teacher and I knew about incidents involving police and family members. We also knew that Beverly was given big responsibilities for very young siblings. The following week we talked, 'in the metaphor', of her certainty that rescue attempts would fail. This encouraged Beverly to speak more openly of nightmares and worries. The teacher was able to reflect on her own experience of irritation and anxiety, freeing her to respond differently in class.

Pessimism about outcomes, illustrated by stories with danger but no chance of rescue, gives a chilling picture of a child's loss of hope about the adult world's capacity to help. A chance, 'at one remove', to think out loud and have this received, digested and challenged, can give relief and encourage further communication and learning.

A NEW PLACE

'A new place' may be an island ahead. Some children are eager to explore; others are wary of potential danger. Drawing their own islands, they exchange ideas.

In Group B, Benton drew a volcano. 'The volcano is all dripping and the trees are all injured. There's a man saying, "Help me!"' Byron echoed this idea and, after making his picture, asked the teacher to write, 'I met a fat woman on the island and I said, "Get on the boat or you'll be dead from the volcano." She doesn't want to be rescued.' Byron was keeping alive a theme from the previous week; a theme he confirmed by drawing a picture entitled 'An angel came to rescue Beverly'. This exemplifies the way in which the joint story 'holds' the group but does not obliterate the individual. Children recognise each other by putting each other into the story. Being heard in this way, by each other and by us, may help children get themselves out of dysfunctional patterns of relating to peers and adults.

Chris, who hated school, didn't want to explore or join in, and irritated everyone with his negative comments about everything. He had drawn solitary computer games to bring on the journey. On the island, as usual he kept saying 'No!' We spoke (in the story) of his 'No!' and suggested that he found it easier to stay in his boat-cabin with his computer than to join in an exploration of the new land. Similar difficulties with joining in hampered Chris' school life. He could infuriate teachers by his gruff refusals, while at home his obsessional use of the computer was used in avoidance of family life, including the fact that his father had not wanted to see him for years. Chris' negativity and avoidance of challenge were named within the context of the story without direct interpretation. He responded by trying out a more 'joining' persona within the story and the group.

THE MYSTERY BOX

A box is 'found' (on a beach, on the moon, in the desert – wherever the journey takes us). It can stand for things known secretly and things not yet known. In families, children may have to keep secrets. Others may feel shut out from knowledge. The box lets us pay attention to these experiences without intrusion. We can talk about where it might have come from, who might own it, what might be inside it and how (or if) we should open it. There may be discussion about locks and keys. It is an opportunity to stay with uncertainty and to encourage hypothesising. An example:

'What's in the box?'
'It could be a treasure chest off Peter Pan.'
'It's a good idea I brought an axe to smash it open.'
'Should we smash it open or leave it?'
'I think we should leave it because it's not ours.'
'It's probably open and it might contain loads of Captain Hook's hooks.'

FALLING OUT

Group D, engaged in making a story about an air balloon, seemed preoccupied with imminent disaster:

We touched the sky.
And then an aeroplane came very near to us.
Mrs M said, 'Oh, what can we do? Has anyone got an idea?'
Dora said, 'Let's try and push it to the side.'
Dot said, 'I don't know!'
Denny said, 'We could jump on to the aeroplane.'

Angus, in a group for the second time, jumped off the balloon saying, 'Goodbye – I die.' Anxiously excited, several group members took this up, repeating it loudly like a chorus.

'What if the aeroplane was right near you and you fell down?' said Darren.
'We could flash the torch on the aeroplane,' said Dora.
'Where has Angus gone? He seems upset today,' said Mrs M.
'He might have fallen out.'
Mr N said, 'Maybe he had a parachute.'
Mrs M said, 'It's hard when someone makes us feel rather worried about them.'
'There he is. He's got a parachute,' said Denny.
'He was standing beside the beach down there,' said Dot.'

Suddenly, Angus ran back to class.
After making sure he was safe, we attempted to think about what had happened.

Mr N said, 'I think we need some rules on our balloon. What rules shall we have?'

Darren said, 'I know. Instead of being scared, be brave and calm.'
'Make sure you eat your food and don't throw it on the aeroplane when you don't like it,' said Denny.
Dora said, 'No swearing or fighting.'

Negative ideas may feel unacceptable to have and dangerous to express directly. In class, nine-year-old Dora often looked exhausted and had a long-standing attendance problem. She was normally silent but one day shared worries with a teacher who took them seriously. Social Services involvement was inconclusive and Dora returned to sad silence and erratic attendance. She had been keeping quiet in the group, only joining in the drawing. Now, tentatively, she had begun to take part in the story.

'Mrs M said, 'I'd like a rule that people listen to each other and try and take turns.'
Denny said, 'We could fall into someone's chimney.'
'It could be full of black coal,' said Darren.
'Or you could fall into a dog's mouth,' said Denny.
'People seem quite worried about falling out of this balloon,' said Mrs M, 'as if the grown-ups wouldn't be able to keep things safe.'

The story that week ended with a discussion about what was seen in the sky in the distance.

'It could be an eagle or another kind of bird,' said Darren.
'It could be a firework or a rocket,' said Dora .
'That's Spyro the dragon,' said Denny.
'I used to ride on him when I was a baby.'

After thinking very hard, shy Doug said very quietly:

'It might be a football, that someone's kicked very, very hard.'
'He must be Bigfoot!' said Denny.
'Or an elephant?' said Darren.
Dora said, 'It could knock us out of the sky or burst us.'
'Maybe it's a flying pig,' said Dot.
'We still don't know where Angus is,' said Mr N.

Angus struggled with his temper when called names, especially since his mother had died the year before. This loss had meant moves between various placements. Now he was living with his father. He had been in

Group A before his mother's death and had made progress prior to that group ending. He had struggled to make sense of things and had, at times, been able to help others in the group think. Yet the subsequent pressure of life events had become overwhelming and now, as a member of Group D, his attempt to leave the balloon and 'fly' back to class in the middle of the session demonstrated this.

Darren's mother had been incapacitated by an illness he did not understand and, knowing that Angus' mother had died, he had joined in eagerly with his noise. Escalating jokey participation (like Angus' 'Goodbye I die') can be a way of expressing worries about family members, especially when children's preoccupations overlap. In an earlier session they had quarrelled and name called. Their family contexts rang bells for each other and led to sparks flying as well as an urge to make reparation after quarrels. The following week the story began with:

'Thank goodness Angus is back with us on the balloon.'
Angus said, 'I don't want to be back. I wish I was in a jungle with crocodiles',

and he drew a vivid picture of this scene with lots of sharp teeth. The following week he arrived distressed. His dad had told him he would be leaving that same day to go to a different school. Angus behaved aggressively, provoking and being provoked by Darren, but after this difficult session he remained behind and burst into tears. Dropping his aggressive stance, he told us, 'My mum put me in this school. Seven years ago!' He felt that he was losing the last bit of her.

GETTING BACK

The boat, balloon or magic carpet has to turn round and get back. Children's expectations about returning home are very different. Will there be a welcome? Will people have survived? Will those who were left behind have forgotten about the child?

Everyone makes a 'postcard' to send home with a name and address, a drawing of something seen on the journey, and a message. Darren chose to make some reparation to Angus, in his absence, for their quarrel by making his postcard:

To
Angus
I hope you like
where you are? from Darren

Darren's reparative card was part of the story, but a real goodbye card was sent by the group wishing Angus well in his new school. We were left feeling that this sudden dislocation in his school life would only strengthen Angus' expectations of disaster and could exacerbate his need to jump before he was dropped.

Choosing time

In competitive games, children can be rivalrous in new ways and can practise managing these feelings through safe rules (Holditch 1995). Doug, often in trouble while trying to be good, usually found it hard to look teachers in the eye but began to do so after the teacher in the group showed him the paper and pencil game of 'Battleships' in which he could safely fight with the teacher (Caspari 1986).

Collaborative activities with construction equipment or drawing and writing games can give a new experience of thinking together. Alvin liked building brick castles. He had been silent until asked to tell a story about his castles for one of the adults to write down. Haltingly, he described the miserable existence of a character who lived in the midst of destruction and violence in a castle inhabited by giants, echoing his mother's description of life at home. Joint story-making (Morton 1996) or 'Squiggle' games (Winnicott 1971b) offer the opportunity to converse, in metaphor, about real worries which cannot yet be spoken about directly. Alice, who had at first struggled to draw or speak, often asked in later sessions for that 'scribbly game' which had helped her to overcome her inhibition about making marks on paper. Dora, silenced by family rules after her attempt to get help for worries about violence and drug-taking, dictated stories of ships and houses destroyed by storms or dangerous creatures. No rescuers ever entered her stories. Without making reference to her circumstances or to the embargo on talking that she appeared to live with, we had conversations about why, in her pictures and stories, no help seemed available, and why someone in the story was not asking for or expecting help.

Some silent children are able to find a voice in the groups, and often the first 'voiced communications' start with 'I hate'. Annie had offered no ideas when asked to make guesses about the story. Her silence was reframed as not feeling ready to share ideas with the group. Missing a turn was allowed but noticed. Some children made guesses about why it might be hard to share an idea with the group – 'she might feel shy', 'she's worried about her mum', 'she don't know', 'she's not well'. In a later group session, Annie unexpectedly joined in a conversation about what was hard in the classroom by saying loudly, 'I hate reading. Reading is crap!' The following week, as I was reading a picture book to the group she placed herself next to me, and my colleague noticed her following the words in a whisper. The 'I hate' of a previously silent child can be a vital first step to learning confidence.

The group offers opportunities to 'contain and digest' (Bion 1967) real worries such as 'my uncle is in prison' or 'my granny is sick' or 'my mum had ten babies but they nearly all died'. There is an opportunity for the children to communicate in a safer way and receive feedback so that they can experience 'making sense'. Denny, for example, had not talked about his father's sudden death. Described by one teacher as being 'a bit obsessional', by another as 'probably a bit deaf', he could get intensely involved with a task, not responding to instructions and unable to stop. His teacher found him frustrating. She never knew if he had heard her. One day, Denny spoke in the group about his father's death, and revealed anxious, muddled ideas about what had happened. We all listened. The next week, at choosing time, he drew and told a muddled story about a monster on an island:

> It's got blue spots and looks kind of black. It's got a black mouth. It's got oil on its mouth. It's got big eyes because it used to be a little thing and a special insect pinched it – a magic one and it spread out and got big eyes. It eats people and when it spits them out it turns into goo and when they turn it into aliens but I'm sure it won't hurt you because I've learned how to communicate with animals and monsters and dinosaurs and stuff.

Denny started mentioning his father in class, made progress with learning and became more in touch with his teacher. His 'cut-off' presentation could be understood as a preoccupation with an important event that left little space for school business.

In or out of the group?

Some children drift over to a window. They point or gaze, and make remarks like 'that's my house', or 'my uncle lives over there'. Others show preoccupation with sounds from inside the school. 'Vigilant' children will think they are needed as soon as they hear any noise either in or out of school and immediately go 'off-task'. Others focus on the table, talking over everyone in a noisy attempt not to be out of the group's mind.

Although wanting to be part of the group, some children, feeling hopeless and unacceptable, prefer to spoil it. Zena, overweight and often excluded from school for aggressive behaviour, tried in the first session to draw herself for the story picture. Dissatisfied with all her efforts, she threw them in the bin and paced around near the windows, making aggravating remarks to the others. Afterwards, my co-worker and I wondered how to help her get started. In the next session, we brought her 'into the picture' by writing her into the story as 'present' but invisible. This freed her to draw herself and to say she'd like to bring an invisible friend on the journey! However, Zena still behaved dangerously by attempting to open a high window, so, as the story was about a journey on a magic carpet, we wrote, 'Zena was worrying everyone on the Magic Carpet when she kept standing near to the edge.' Showing interest, she came nearer to the table.

At choosing time, Zena urgently wanted paper to make a book but couldn't get beyond her first sentence, 'Once there was a worst sister . . . ' (her sister had managed much better at school) which she had written and crossed out. She then spent the rest of the time deriding the efforts of others. Her 'book', lacking contents, seemed an external expression of a hopeless inner picture of self. She wanted to join the group but couldn't quite get started and her behaviour seemed an avoidance of painful thinking.

Although therapeutic groupwork can be a useful opportunity for many children, it can prove intolerable for others – tantalising because of the wish to join, yet awful because of the fear of being unacceptable. Behaviour in the group may illustrate the need for further intervention such as individual educational therapy, counselling sessions in school or, as in Zena's case, a referral to other agencies.

Impact, outcomes and conclusions

Therapeutic groupwork of the kind described here has two aims: first, to provide children with a space for some 'containment' and 'digestion' of unmanageable feelings; second, to provide space for teachers to develop their observation and reflection skills in relation to vulnerable children and to increase their therapeutic repertoires.

In relation to the first aim, the clinical material illustrates how, initially, the nature of the space provided – being separate from but not in opposition to school – is marked out by using introductory games which show children that difficulties will be thought about, at times challenged rather than confronted, and that adults will remain in charge of safety and structure. Gradually, the reliability of the space is confirmed by our (the leaders') attitude of respectful, non-intrusive listening in which we 'hold' and 'digest' communications rather than reject or react to them. Within this distinctive, reliable space, the evolving story includes each child's ideas while safeguarding each child's individuality, thus giving them the chance to feel part of something as well as being recognised as separate from it. These characteristics – intimacy and distance, connectedness and separateness – allow children who have been forced to live with an embargo on talking about their distress to find, through metaphor, a voice: an opportunity to think the unthinkable and to express what they think. In turn, this may rekindle enough hope about being heard and about the possibility of change, so that they may feel it is possible to let others know about significant worries in a clearer way than through disruptive behaviour or learning difficulties.

With regard to the second aim – that of staff development – teacher involvement in the selection and running of the groups helps to promote this. Before, during and after the groups, as original concerns are reviewed and teachers are offered strategies that have helped the child in the group, thinking goes on.

Teachers can observe and think about children's ways of communicating distress more easily when they are with children without being solely in charge. They can feel more skilled and less at the mercy of children's feelings (often expressed in disruptive or withdrawn behaviour). Indeed, just as working therapeutically with the educational context can help shift an unhelpful pattern of 'child against teacher', so can working with parents, teachers and children help shift a pattern of 'home against school'. In this way, everyone can feel part of a process of joined-up thinking and owners of a change for the better.

Note

1 Later, parents are also asked for views and offered a chance to raise questions.

References

Barrett, M. and Trevitt, J. (1991) *Attachment Behaviour and the School Child*, London: Routledge.

Bion, W. (1962) 'A theory of thinking', in *Second Thoughts*, London: Karnac, 1984.

—— (1967) 'Learning from experience', in *Second Thoughts*, London: Karnac, 1984.

Bowlby J. (1988) *A Secure Base: Clinical Applications of Attachment Theory*, London: Tavistock.

Caspari, I. (1986) *The Collected Papers*, London: Tavistock.

Dawson, N. and MacHugh, B. (1994) 'Parents and children: participants in change', in E. Dowling and E. Osborne (eds) *The Family and the School: A Joint Systems Approach to Problems with Children*, London: Routledge.

Dover-Councell, J. (1997) 'Educational therapy', *Young Minds Bulletin Magazine*, 28.

Dyke, S. (1987) 'Psychoanalytic insight in the classroom: asset or liability?', *Journal of Educational Therapy*, 1(4): 43–63.

Freud, S. (1912) 'The dynamics of transference', in *The Standard Edition*, Vol. 12, London: Hogarth Press, 1958.

Holditch, L. (1995) 'Learning: only a game?', *Journal of Educational Therapy*, 1(4): 34–43.

Morton, G. (1996) 'The therapeutic potential of storymaking', *Educational Therapy and Therapeutic Teaching*, 5, London: FAETT.

Salzberger-Wittenberg, I., Henry, G. and Osborne, E. (1983) *The Emotional Experience of Learning and Teaching*, London: Routledge & Kegan Paul.

Watzlawick, P., Weakland, J. and Fisch, R. (1974) *Change: Principles of Problem Formation and Problem Resolution*, New York: Norton.

White, M. (1988/89) 'The externalising of the problem and the re-authoring of lives and relationships', *Dulwich Centre Newsletter*, Summer 1988/89.

Winnicott, D. W. (1960) 'The theory of the parent–infant relationship', in *The Maturational Processes and the Facilitating Environment: Studies in the Theory of Emotional Development*, London: Karnac, 1990.

—— (1971a) *Playing and Reality*, London: Tavistock.

—— (1971b) *Therapeutic Consultations in Child Psychiatry*, London: Hogarth Press.

Chapter 11

Loss, creativity and leaving home

Investigating adolescent essay anxiety

Nick Barwick

Introduction

At the heart of the institutional educational process is writing, and the form of writing given most credence in academic circles is the essay. Almost as common as the essay is the anxiety that accompanies it.

Although counselling now forms the main body of my work, I have taught A-level English for fifteen years and have been struck by how many students fail to fulfil their academic potential because of essay-writing anxiety. As a teacher, I have spent considerable time explaining the mechanics of essay production. Often such explanations have sufficed. Yet often they have not. In such instances, I, as much as the student, have been left with a sense of frustration, impotence, despair. It has been the frequent failure of this essentially cognitive approach, together with the uncomfortable residue of feelings that have accompanied it, that has prompted me to investigate students' essay-writing difficulties with psychodynamic rather than pedagogic eyes.

The context from which the case material used in this chapter is drawn is a sixth-form college. Employed originally as a teacher, I helped to establish a counselling service there, of which I became the first paid member. As the service grew and non-teaching staff replaced myself and the voluntary counsellors, I returned to a teaching role within the institution. For some time, however, colleagues continued to approach me about 'problem' students, including those who appeared to be underachieving. It was as a psychodynamically informed teacher then, with historical links to the counselling service, that I undertook the investigations upon which this chapter is based.

Investigative counselling

I use the term investigative counselling because of what was, at that time, the dual nature of my aims – to investigate some of the sources of essay anxiety and, if possible, to alleviate student distress. The compatibility of these aims may seem questionable. The former foregrounds the interests of the researcher, the latter the individual researched upon. However, psychodynamic investigation demands that the researcher undertakes affective as well as cognitive processing of client material (Heimann 1950), and since it can be argued that the resultant act of empathic understanding brings some relief (see e.g. Bion 1962; Segal 1975; even more explicitly see Kohut 1984; Wolf 1991), investigative and therapeutic aims tend, within the psychodynamic field, to be complementary. Indeed, in my experience, counselling work which has an investigative focus on a student's specific educational 'hitch' can not only have a rapid remedial effect on those difficulties but can also offer fruitful and relatively unthreatening ways of beginning to explore the deeper 'hitch in the individual's emotional development' (Winnicott 1986).

Further benefits of the investigative approach are:

1   it is in keeping with the educational ethos at A level;
2   it is less of a threat to the adolescent drive for independence.

In short, it is more acceptable to many students to put themselves forward as research subjects than it is to ask for help. Thus my use of open letters outlining the field of investigation – given to students via their teachers – the issuing of questionnaires for respondents and a brief initial discussion explaining the collaborative nature of the venture – *my* investigation which might for *them* have some beneficial effect – brought interest from students who might otherwise not have found their way to counselling.

With a contract of five forty-five-minute sessions agreed,[1] each session maintained a clear focus: the student's relationship with the essay. Although encouraging free association – the student's proffering of relatively uncensored thoughts and images – I ensured that that focus was never far from mind. As for the transference (see Chapter 4), I encouraged an exploration of this in relation to the essay. For example, did their way of relating to the essay – their feelings about it – echo their relationship and feelings about anything or anyone else? However, I avoided 'gathering' the transference (Meltzer 1968) – a process by which the relationship between client and counsellor becomes central and ever more emotionally charged – and refrained from transference interpretations –

those interpretations focusing on the client's way of relating to the counsellor. Thus, these sessions, in their guided use of focus, their employment of selective interpretation, attention and neglect, have much in common with certain models of brief dynamic therapy (e.g. Malan 1976), while the restrained use of the transference matches well the approach often advocated by therapists working with adolescents (e.g. Wilson 1991).

Theory in context

Textual relations

My only criterion for selecting students was that they perceived *themselves* as suffering from essay anxiety and that their teachers perceived them as being moderately to very able. The fact that they were able suggested that the anxiety aroused in them by the prospect of an essay owed at least as much to the state of their internal worlds as the objective status of the essay itself. True, the essay, being rigorous in its demands and insistent on certain academic mores, can *appear* authoritative and *be* inhibitive (Barwick 1988). Nevertheless, no matter how liberal the teacher or how encouraging her remarks about the desirability of rumination and play, a student's essay anxiety is never easily assuaged. I believe a major reason why essay anxiety appears so intransigent is that it is rooted not only in a student's relationship with what lies ahead (the essay) but also in the relationship with what has been left behind (the literary or 'mother text' being studied).

To suggest that a student has a relationship with an essay may seem curious. That he or she has a relationship with a 'mother text' may seem even more so. In using such language, however, I am drawing upon one of the dominant strands of contemporary psychoanalytic thought, namely object relations.

The term 'object' refers here to a thing, person or idea about which we have feelings and to which we therefore relate. The earliest 'whole object' a baby relates to is the primary care giver/mother, also known as 'primary object'; the earliest 'part object' is the breast. Part objects are not physically perceived but experienced emotionally through the body (Bion 1959). Thus a baby who, on feeling the first pangs of hunger, soon experiences the presence of a satisfying feed – one which attends to both material and emotional needs – takes in (introjects) that experience of the breast as 'good object'. Over time, such introjection builds certain expectations: that whenever hunger comes, so too will relief. Conversely, a baby who does not experience such timely comfort may introject the experience of the breast as 'bad object', giving rise to expectations characterised not by hope but fear. Of course, as we grow older, we leave the breast behind. Yet we never entirely relinquish the relational script – that is, our expectations about relationships – which is its legacy. It is this point that I am trying to highlight by using the term 'mother text' – the literary text from which the student, prior to producing an essay, feeds.

The activity of learning (Klein 1931; Salzberger-Wittenberg *et al.* 1983), and by association reading (Strachey 1930), can be seen to be intimately related to our early experience at the breast. Indeed the connection is so strong that it permeates the very metaphors we use. We talk about being 'greedy' for knowledge. We 'consume' and 'devour' books. We 'chew' over thoughts, 'digest' concepts, 'regurgitate' some ideas, 'swallow' others, while 'distasteful', 'indigestible' or 'poisonous' ones can 'make us sick'. Thus, although the act of study is sophisticated, requiring complex cognitive functioning, it is underpinned by primitive (that is, early) ways of thinking and relating, full of primitive hopes, fears and expectations. Since, generally, we are unaware of the manner in which such expectations colour our perceptions and behaviours, and since these expectations, being old and out of date, are often unrelated to the reality of the situation, they are referred to as 'unconscious phantasies' (Isaacs 1948).

In writing an essay, students must do more than feed. Having imbibed the 'mother text', they must take their place as independent practitioners – ones who produce rather than consume. In doing so, they must bear the loss of the 'mother text'. More accurately, they must bear its transformation, since the text produced must be born out of the digested parts of the text consumed.

The student/baby's experience of loss is complex, since neither feeding nor digestion are passive processes. The mouth presses against the nipple. It sucks. It bites. Further, once the milk is in the stomach, digestive juices attack it, invade it, break it down. This process is creative – food is assimilated and the baby grows – but it is also aggressive. So too with students who 'get their teeth' into a text. They are required to 'enter into it', to 'pull it to pieces' and in the name of educational development, to make it their own. However, while creative use of aggression may bring succour of personalised knowledge, phantasies arising from unconscious recognition of aggression's destructive nature may also bring anxieties of guilt (Joseph 1978; Klein 1935).

Guilt may spur the individual to new acts of potency and symbolic repair (Klein 1937; Segal 1952, 1991): the greedy baby strokes the breast; the 'naughty' child makes a present for her mother; the pining artist paints a picture, and the literature student, having analysed the 'mother text' to near death, writes an essay. Yet if, in phantasy, aggression is perceived as irretrievably damaging, loss resulting from the attack on the 'good object' (the breast/the mother text) is seen not as potentially transformative but absolute. With no reparation possible, guilt proffers not hope of reparation but creative impotence and despair.

How aggression is experienced by baby or student depends on experiences of containment (Bion 1962). For the baby, containment describes a process that forms part of healthy mother–infant relations. The wordless infant, unable to make sense of its feelings – among them aggression – projects (gets rid of) them into the mother. If she can allow these primitive communications to penetrate her, and if she can tolerate their assault, their meaning may gradually emerge. On the basis of this meaning she can respond. In this way, the infant learns that feelings (like aggression) are not overly dangerous, but can be thought about and creatively used. A mother, however, who is unable to take in such intense projections, or while taking them in is overwhelmed, communicates the opposite: that such feelings are too dangerous to be thought about and cannot be constructively used. Babies who are left with such uncontained feelings simultaneously deny these 'bad objects' in themselves and intensify their projection of them into the environment.

Many students gripped by intellectual paralysis are, I believe, haunted by uncontained feelings of aggression. That many are prone to depression seems to confirm a fear of aggressive impulses; impulses which, denied in themselves, are projected into the environment, further feeding the phantasy of persecutory essays and essay assessors. Others, though producing, bring shameful confessions about the 'good object' they fear they have spoiled. 'It's crap', they say. It should follow that students not thus hampered will experience little essay anxiety. However, I am not sure this is so. I think this is because, especially in adolescence, successful creation of an essay may lead to further losses and attendant anxieties – ones which arise from the assertion of an independent mind. Students may not yet be prepared to sanction these.

In adolescence, as the body acquires adult potency, curiosity and its ally, independent, creative, original thought are not only aggressive but sexualised. As Wooster (1986) points out, the Hebrew word for knowledge – *da'at* – is rooted in sex. Thus, phantasies about 'entering', 'devouring' and 'knowing' the text and then conceiving an essay may, at an unconscious level, give rise to disturbing phantasies about parental jealousy, envy and retribution (see Chapter 1 on the Oedipus complex). This, after all, is how it was for the first adolescents. Adam and Eve, feeding from the Tree of Knowledge – committing thereby both original thought and sin – first became sexually excited, then fearful, then ashamed. Fearful, they hid from the Father. The fear, of course, was worse than the reality. Although innocent dependence *was* lost, Adam and Eve were neither destroyed nor entirely abandoned. They were simply asked to move out of the parental home.

Yet leaving home is no mean feat. Home is indeed where the heart is, and unless the good object of 'home' has been satisfyingly integrated, adolescents who try to leave do so emotionally anaemic. In fact, an irony I have noticed is that those students who suffer most from essay anxiety are those who seem most desperate to move away from home. As if unconsciously recognising the essay as symbol of intellectual and emotional independence, it is the essay they refuse to produce. Thus the frustrated vigour of each step forward forces them, paradoxically, to look back.

Clinical work

The non-starter

Sarah, a nervy sixteen-year-old, spoke in rapid bursts. Having written only one essay in six months, she expressed her difficulties thus:

> 'I sat trying desperately to write. . . . A strange hopelessness . . . grabbed my thoughts, sapping my knowledge, leaving me a helpless relic of former glory.'

Creative impotence seemed explicit, as did the mourning of what was lost. Yet in our meetings, omnipotence – often used as a defence against painful feelings of powerlessness and need – was more often the keynote. She had no doubt, she said, that she could write essays, if only she were motivated. She simply saw 'no point'.

My countertransference – my feelings about Sarah – matched the contradictory nature of her presentation. At times I felt drawn to soothe what seemed to be her isolation, her despair. When teachers saw she couldn't write an essay, they talked only of planning. They never asked why. Anger was barely concealed. So was unmet need. Yet when I tried to explore what essay anxiety meant for her, she responded with contempt. She thought it amazing that I analysed everything. She didn't write essays because she didn't write essays! Quite simply, I felt stupid. Shamefully, I also felt a strong urge to retaliate – to burst her pompous, self-opinionated air.

Bion (1958) comments that the triad of arrogance, stupidity and curiosity indicates a primitive mental catastrophe: a breakdown in empathic communion between infant and primary object. Sarah, in her attempts to find out more about me and her evident irritation at my refusal to be drawn, signalled intense curiosity, while the more I tried to offer in terms of understanding, the more useless and stupid I felt with every arrogant rebuff. If, in the transference, I represented the primary object, was the hunger she felt for contact frustrating her beyond endurance? Was her apparent arrogance a sign of an omnipotently conjured ability to feed herself; one which gave her the illusion of feeling replete while in reality she starved? If so, no wonder, when I *did* manage to offer food for thought, scornfully, she turned away.

Later meetings threw further light on my desire to attack. She talked about her experience of being bullied at school. 'I think it was because of my squint', she said. It crossed my mind whether the attacks focused on her, both by peers and myself, might not have been to some extent stimulated by the intense projection of her own uncontained aggression. Further, since her attacks were oblique/squinted, was there a fear of the damage she might wreak should her assault be more focused?

Sarah's teacher commented on her 'lack of organisation' and her 'inability to focus'. Yet this was not quite true. Sarah could focus, but only in another's presence. For example, she talked fondly of her old English teacher and his struggle to get her to write a 'controlled essay': 'He managed to pin me down . . . and get me to do it.'

The desire for confinement was something Sarah frequently referred to: 'I need someone to push me'; 'I need to feel pressured'; even 'I found detention very helpful. You do a lot of work.' It was when she had no 'point' of pressure, no resilient containment, that she floundered:

> 'Jane [her new teacher] went through the essay with me and it all made perfect sense. When I got home though, it didn't. I just went blank.'

If they wrote essays in class she was 'OK'. But to be given the question and then 'left with it! Where was the point in that?'

For Sarah, when the 'point' was absent, what was present was the badness of 'it' – not only the persecutory question but the contents of her own mind. It was as if Sarah's curiosity, imbued as it was with uncontained, unmodified aggression, had to be nullified for fear of the irreparable damage it could wreak. To focus or organise her thoughts, to engage without the containing presence of another, was so anxiety provoking that it was unthinkable. Her answer? To evacuate ('blank') her mind.

In the last two meetings, Sarah explicitly mentioned unwanted, 'morbid thoughts'. These, together with her reference to herself as a 'relic', and her description of me as vulture-like, 'picking over my [her] thoughts', suggested that she was 'much possessed by death' (Eliot 1920). A further defence against such possession were her 'normal thoughts' to which, at the end of meetings, she was keen to return. These included contempt for what English and college had to offer, certainty in her academic ability, and dreams of independence.

Sarah appeared frustrated at being unable to move towards independence. Yet she also recognised that, by not writing, it was her movement forward that she prevented:

> 'The importance of these questions struck home. . . . My future depended upon the movements of my pen. . . . I am not getting anywhere. I never do. . . . I have gone backwards.'

Even after what seemed to be very productive meetings, she offered, as her parting gift, very similar words – 'We don't get anywhere, do we?' By means of this passing shot, not only did she deny the value of what I had given – releasing her from painful desire and need – but she sought to try and engage me further. In effect, while she dismissed the 'home' she was leaving, unconsciously it was *at* 'home' that she really wanted to stay.

Sarah spoke of home relatively little. What she said suggested that she and her parents occupied different worlds. Her feelings towards them were typically ambivalent, welcoming the freedom they gave her – 'They let me do what I want' – yet resenting the lack of touch – 'Why don't they push me more?' She had not consulted them about quitting college – 'They've got a lot to think about' – just as she had not consulted them about coming to our college. She had had to consult them about her original plan – to go elsewhere. If she had got a place, it would have meant them paying. However, having failed to get accepted at her ideal college, she drifted into ours:

> 'If I'd gone to ——, I'd've been alright. I would've had to work because my parents would've been paying. I would've been motivated.'

Payment thus milked from her parents would have been a demonstration of care. With such care, she could have proffered work as reward. I asked her what her refusal to work might mean. It was a question she struggled to ignore. In the end she answered, 'I guess I'm saying, if you'd pushed me, it wouldn't be like this.' For 'push' we might read 'contained': the firmness of parental boundaries around the wilful, murderous adolescent; the resolute pressure of nipple upon the infant's lips despite aggression mobilised by teething gums.

Sarah felt intensely uncomfortable about the thought of what she might be communicating and her method of doing it. 'But why should I want to hurt myself?' Then, out of nowhere, she added, 'Perhaps that's why some people commit suicide?' Wincing at her own remark, she repressed it. 'Uuggh!' she grimaced, 'I don't want to think – .'

It was not a physical suicide that she was trying to commit however, but an educational one:

> 'After my GCSEs, there was no pressure. I felt really empty, depressed. I didn't do anything for six months except stay in bed. Nobody noticed.'

GCSEs and the move to college marked steps towards independence. Yet such independence, for Sarah, was premature. In its prematurity, it echoed her experience of earlier separations, where loss had occurred at points of heightened, uncontained aggression and where new independence had left her similarly 'empty': the unmodified phantasy of the decimated parent behind her matching the absence of the good object/'point' within.

Although Sarah had physically risen from bed to come to college, academically she had not. Someone 'noticed' only six months in. Ironically, the college's response was first to reduce the 'pressure' of three A levels to two and, when that failed, to inform her that though she could consider returning to study for another year, in her present state of mind there really seemed to be 'no point'.

The non-completer

At age nineteen, Kevin was older than most second years. His first year saw erratic production of promising work. His second saw very little, and none of it complete.

> 'When I . . . start an essay I always feel very apprehensive. . . . I get . . . tense. . . . I end up getting angry with . . . myself, because I can't express myself and I feel like I've failed.'

Failure to 'express' signalled impotence. Angry at such failure, he turned against himself – the result: frustration, illness, depression. Only gradually did another anger emerge: 'I feel angry too because it [writing] was always something I enjoyed.'

Kevin spoke of his relationship with writing like a disappointed lover: 'I feel distanced', 'uninvolved'. Soon pining gave way to complaint. He described the essay as 'insensitive', 'ungiving'; the organisation and planning it demanded was 'uncreative'. He added, 'I don't feel that the essay can hold my feelings. I don't want to give my feelings up to it. They'd get lost.'

When writing an essay, he often had a thought and turned to the computer, only to find that the thought had gone. I asked him if he made notes. 'Never. If I did, all I'd be left with would be words. Nothing would be left in them.' The essay, and all that preceded it, seemed to threaten to devour the good object – his 'feelings' – which he held inside.

Kevin's description of the essay as a restrictive, insensitive, devouring container applied equally to his experience of home. He had to share a bedroom with his elder brother. There was no space to work. Further, his elder brother, hyperactive and prone to angry fits, was the focus of his mother's attentions. In contrast, her relationship with Kevin was manipulative and controlling:

> 'She seems to do things for you, but she doesn't. She seems to give, but she takes. I wish she could read how I felt. I try and say how I feel but she just picks it up, tells me what I mean and dismisses it.'

With a mother ignorant of his needs, a withdrawn, placid father, and a younger sister for whom he felt responsible, there simply was no space to 'express' his feelings, especially those of anger.

Kevin found keeping anger in check wearing, though he managed it well. His unassuming disposition, quiet voice and thoughtful approach made it easy to warm to him. Yet, as if to warn me, biting his bottom lip – a frequent gesture – he commented, 'My friends and family see me as calm, organized. Inside I'm not.' I asked him what was 'inside'. Again the lip: 'I don't know . . . I . . . I . . . I. . . . ' His speech, always intense, gave way to inarticulateness. I felt impotent to help. When next I saw him, he told me that after our meeting he had gone home and 'puked up'.

It occurred to me that Kevin's complaint about the inadequate container – mother, home, essay, words, me – was not only a comment on how unsafe he felt when faced with its greedy insensitivity, but how unsafe the container might be were he to allow himself to enter it in a manner befitting his need. Perhaps his finer feeling, which felt too precious to cast into such a container, was a defence against a deeper fear: the fear that the mess which lay 'inside' him was too caustic to be contained. This made me think again about his initial complaint – impotence in the face of the essay. If the essay, as potential container, had become somehow muddled in his mind with his mother, could impotence be a defence not only against the 'expression' of caustic messiness but against sexualised aggression?

As Kevin explored more freely both his anger against and need for his mother, his approach to essays changed dramatically. Able to disentangle anger from the essay, he found that he could think about writing without running away. Attacking the essay container with zest, within the next two months he wrote all the essays required to complete the coursework element, consistently achieving B and A grades. Or rather, he completed all essays bar one.

As Kevin approached the end of his time at college, the assertion of potent, independent manhood had ever greater appeal. He would not be like his elder brother who still lived at home. He would not be like his father, kindly but 'put upon'. Still, in our last meeting, a story he related about youthful cycling ventures indicated his ambivalence about asserting such potency:

'Mum told me I wasn't to go beyond a certain point. All my friends did . . . so I did too. When mum found out, she was really angry. She told me never to do it again. I did. I kept on doing it. She never understood why I wanted to go. She just gave up. I don't want an ending like that. There's so much lost.'

Kevin was fearful of the impotence inherent in remaining at home. Yet it was difficult to leave when what he needed most he felt he had not got – a quality of preoccupation, of understanding, of intimacy. Further, it was as if his prolonged bid for freedom – be it a repetitive cycle ride or lingering one essay past the deadline – was not only an attempt to coax his mother into 'reading' him but a call to arms; an effort to engage his mother in sustained conflict, in the unconscious hope that thereby his aggressive impulses might at last be acknowledged, understood, contained.

Yet his mother, preoccupied with the activities of her other son, appeared unable to know him in this way. Her premature abdication denied him the experience of creativity born out of aggressive conflict, leaving him, to some extent, still wary of his own potency, reluctantly holding on to what he had never had. And here is an irony that haunts all our struggles to grow: for that *from* which we feel most reluctant to separate is that *of* which we have never felt a part.

The non-exhibitor

Katrina, a pale, freckled, first year, looking a good two years younger than her age, wrote of essay writing:

> 'I make too many notes but I don't feel I have enough. . . . I feel that the essay will be bad . . . I dread the essay. . . . I worry about what I write. Does it sound right? . . . Everything I write feels awful, even if it is sound work. I've missed every deadline so far.'

Katrina had no difficulty in 'taking in'. Compulsively she fed on everything, though it never seemed enough. This made her wary of producing. However, she *did* produce and *did*, eventually, complete. What she completed however were essays of industry, copious and careful, in which, according to her teacher, 'she cannot see the wood for the trees'. Her meticulous repetition of all the teacher gave her – an obsessional regurgitation to match her obsessional taking in – had helped her to achieve GCSE success. At A level, where independent thought was required, it had not.

The manner of our meetings matched the manner of her study. I found her attentive, compliant, peculiarly insubstantial. At our first encounter, she refrained from any utterance exceeding a couple of words for fear, she eventually said, of sounding 'stupid'. For the most part, I felt drawn to intuit what she felt, then articulate it. She responded with a nod if she agreed, long silences if she was not sure. She never shook her head or openly dismissed an idea.

What Katrina seemed scared of producing was her own mess. She feared contaminating the goodness of anything imbibed. Even though she recognised her work as 'sound' – an odd, 'teacherly' term to use about her own creation – it still '*felt* awful'. It felt awful because she recognised that no matter how hard she tried, she could not keep the good object introjected insulated from her own contaminating desires. Yet it felt awful too, I think, because the object alone did not satisfy her. In other words, the essay's awfulness arose not because it was messy – being 'sound' it was patently not – but because it was a sham.

Her comment on her choice of questions confirmed as much:

'I always feel I've chosen wrong. I choose the one that's safe. There's probably another one I'm more interested in but don't take, in case I sound stupid.'

Another 'voice' yearned to risk, to reveal.

Katrina talked more of this 'other voice'. Apparently she enjoyed singing and did so at competition level. She had also done GCSE drama, another area of 'performance' she loved. Again the conflict between desire and inhibition was striking – 'In improvisation I'd have an idea but I could never get the confidence to go into the circle and do it. I'd just sit on the edge of my chair' – as was the image of penetrating the circle to perform. Again, in scripted plays, though she took 'small parts', she fantasised about 'big ones', while in the weeks when I saw her she went further, joining an amateur dramatic society.

Accompanying our exploration of her dramatic voice, I asked Katrina to think about her censorious one. Was it like any external voice she had heard? Her answer was 'Yes, my dad's'. Katrina described her relationship with him as close, until she reached the age of twelve. Then they had drifted apart. Since GCSEs, it had got worse. His jokes appeared more cruel, his comments more 'sarky', 'cutting' – words also used to describe her teacher's 'wounding' comments about her essays. Though normally she did not respond to her father, at times, anger, which had been 'bubbling up', suddenly 'exploded'. I said that though this sounded dangerous it also sounded energetic, exciting even. I ventured further. And as I steeled myself to do so, I felt anxiety rise. Would I break the bounds of decorum?

'Perhaps your dad has difficulty in accepting you as a young, sexually mature woman?'

Silence. I thought she was going to ignore the comment, withdraw. Instead, she replied with peculiar clarity. 'I think he still wants me to be his little girl.'

A uniquely fluent piece of articulation followed. She talked of how he did not seem to like her going out at night; of how he would tell her that what she wore was 'too revealing'. It made her feel embarrassed – uncertain whether she was 'showing too much'. Still, she said with a smile that she was learning to 'handle it' – and him I presumed – and had recently begun to go out without feeling she had to conform.

This was exactly what she began to do with her essays. As she began to delight in her own body, so too did she begin to delight in her own mind. Three weeks after our initial meeting, she produced her first successful essay – a B/A. True, its production came only after a great deal of to-ing and fro-ing. As her teacher commented, 'She seems to need her hand holding each step of the way.' None the less, she had made a breakthrough. Further, it was to my own delight that, at our final meeting, she told me that with another essay deadline set, though all the old 'dread' had come to the fore, she was already well on her way to producing. In her own penetrating words, 'I thought rather than just sitting on the edge dreading it, I'd plunge in.'

Conclusion: 'What remains'

One student, middle-aged rather than adolescent, when asked whether she had started an essay, replied, 'I don't want to. I don't want to open Pandora's box.' There are two versions of this myth; two versions of what the box contains. In one, it holds all human ills; in another, all the blessings of the gods. The same box, the same essay. The contents depend upon who the story-teller is. And yet, even for the writer/teller expecting blessings, there is the inevitable twist, for when the box was opened, all blessings escaped, all lost; all, that is, except hope.

It is the degree of hope – a trust that 'what remains' (Wordsworth 1804), though never quite enough, will do – that marks the difference between the writer who manages to contain the anxiety of loss and the writer who does not. This hope and this containment is dependent partly upon the writer's own experience of hope and containment in early infancy, and in an inevitably interrelated way, on the creative ability to utilise aggression. I have suggested that these factors are given new meaning in adolescence. Yet, in a fashion, every student faced with an essay is both infant and adolescent, since to write an essay is to enter into the process of individuation (Blos 1967; Mahler 1968); a developmental process in which each venturer, in bearing the loss inherent in separation, is faced with the potential freedom and catastrophe of change.

Note

1   I reminded students that if they wished to explore issues further, they could use the counselling service. A few took up this opportunity.

References

Barwick, N. (1988) *Responding to Literature: Towards A New Authority* (unpublished MA thesis), University of Sussex.

Bion, W. R. (1958) 'On arrogance', in *Second Thoughts*, London: Karnac, 1984.

—— (1959) 'Attacks on linking', in *Second Thoughts*, London: Karnac, 1984.

—— (1962) 'A theory of thinking', in *Second Thoughts*, London: Karnac, 1984.

Blos, P. (1967) 'The second individuation process of adolescence', *The Psychoanalytic Study of the Child*, 22: 162–186.

Eliot, T. S. (1920) 'Whispers of Immortality', in *The Complete Poems and Plays*, London: Faber and Faber, 1978.

Heimann, P. (1950) 'On counter-transference', *International Journal of Psycho-Analysis*, 31: 81–84.

Isaacs, S. (1948) 'The nature and function of phantasy', in Melanie Klein, Paula Heimann, Susan Isaacs and Joan Riviere (eds) *Developments in Psycho-Analysis*, London: The Hogarth Press and the Institute of Psycho-Analysis, 1952.

Joseph, B. (1978) 'Different types of anxiety and their handling in the analytic situation', *International Journal of Psycho-Analysis*, 59: 223–228.

Klein, M. (1931) 'A contribution to the theory of intellectual inhibition', in *Love, Guilt and Reparation and Other Works 1921–1945*, London: Virago Press, 1988.

—— (1935) 'A contribution to the psychogenesis of manic-depressive states', in *Love, Guilt and Reparation and Other Works 1921–1945*, London: Virago Press, 1988.

—— (1937) 'Love, guilt and reparation', in *Love, Guilt and Reparation and other Works 1921–1945*, London: Virago Press, 1988.

Kohut, H. (1984) *How Does Analysis Cure?*, Chicago, IL: University of Chicago Press.

Mahler, M. (1968) *On Human Symbiosis and the Vicissitudes of Individuation: Infantile Psyches*, New York: International Universities Press.

Malan, D. H. (1976) *The Frontier of Brief Psychotherapy*, New York: Plenum.

Meltzer, D. (1968) *The Psycho-Analytic Process*, Perth: Clunie.

Salzberger-Wittenberg, I., Henry, G. and Osborne, E. (1983) *The Emotional Experience of Learning and Teaching*, London: Routledge.

Segal, H. (1952) 'Psycho-analytic approach to aesthetics', in *The Work of Hanna Segal*, London: Free Association Books, 1986.

—— (1975) 'A psycho-analytic approach to the treatment of schizophrenia', in *The Work of Hanna Segal*, London: Free Association Books, 1986.

—— (1991) *Dream, Phantasy and Art*, London: Tavistock.

Strachey, J. (1930) 'Some unconscious factors in reading', *International Journal of Psycho-Analysis*, 11.

Wilson, P. (1991) 'Psychotherapy with adolescents', in J. Holmes (ed.) *Textbook of Psychotherapy in Psychiatric Practice*, Edinburgh: Churchill Livingstone.

Winnicott, D. W. (1986) *Home is Where we Start from*, London: Pelican.

Wolf, E. S. (1991) 'Advances in self psychology: the evolution of psycho-analytic treatment', *Psychoanalytic Inquiry*, 11: 123–146.

Wooster, G. (1986) 'Working psychotherapeutically in a student health setting', *Psychoanalytic Psychotherapy*, 2(2): 99–110.

Wordsworth, W. (1804) 'Intimations of Immortality from Recollections of Early Childhood', in *The Selected Poetry and Prose of Wordsworth*, ed. G. H. Hartman, New York: Signet Classics, 1970.

Index

abandonment 10, 29, 81, 92, 113
abilities 124
absolutism 128, 163
abuse 13, 81, 94; sexual 97; shouted at teachers 109
accommodation 98, 112
ACE (Advisory Centre for Education) 66
achievement 71, 142, 143
acting out 18, 41, 57
adaptation 26, 98; mothers' degree of 23–4
adolescence 11, 14, 109, 111; difficulties 18–20; dominant feature of 53; early 15–16; essay anxiety 159–74; in groups 16, 17, 18, 19; later 16–17; learning in 12, 17–18
adoption 10
affection 77, 78, 91
affective domain 124
aggression 72, 73, 74, 78, 84, 91, 121, 153; creative use of 162, 172; exclusion for 156; loud and flamboyant 93; sexualised 169; uncontained 163, 165, 167
Ainsworth, M. D. 82
ambivalence 17, 43, 62, 70, 83, 91, 169; towards parents 166
anger 41, 45, 48, 58, 60, 74, 76, 83, 92; coping with 75; disentangled from essay 169; drawings representing 116; exploded 171;

keeping in check 168; rooted in conclusions 120; viewed as *secondary emotion* 126 *see also* anger management
anger management 118, 124–41
annihilation 49
antisocial behaviour 41; *see also* behavioural difficulties
anxiety 26, 27, 28, 44, 77, 84, 93, 94, 96, 98; articulating 66; assuaging 82, 161; communicating 78; contained 82; defending against 24, 62, 143; essay-writing 159–74; 'full up' with 81; group 137; incomprehensible 67; level of 101; measuring the degree of 100; Oedipal 74; panic and 85; practitioners' 39–40; preoccupation with 82; reliable attachment figure who can think through 83; revealed 69; surmounting 53
appearance 53; unkempt 71
approval 49, 135, 136
arbitrary inference 103
arousal 67, 68
arrogance 165
art 26–8, 89, 108–23
assessment 42, 99; art and play in 115–17; formulation and 100–2
assimilation 98, 162
assumptions 98, 103, 114; maladaptive 128; negative 112
attachments 82–4, 85, 91, 92, 93, 143;

91; fear of 78; 'inappropriate
closure' to 120
constructions 60
contact 71, 72, 76, 77, 92; craving 91
containers 67, 89, 168–9
containment 18, 19, 68, 73, 78, 86,
136, 143; aggression and 163;
early infancy 172; inadequate 9;
opportunities for 155; space for
156
context 144
contracts 43
control 76, 84, 89, 91, 168; losing 53,
134; omnipotent 77
coping 63, 76, 100; with anger 75;
with conflict 120; with curiosity
75; with pain 81, 88
core conditions 38, 39
Coren, Alex 17
countertransference 54, 55, 57, 58,
68, 76, 164; manifestations of 73
creativity 27, 30, 83, 111, 159–74
criticism 74, 102
cruelty 89
CRUSE (bereavement charity) 120
cues 75
curiosity 8, 9, 10, 72, 82, 163; coping
with 75; intense 165; lack of 6
curriculum 69, 75, 76, 77, 85, 99,
143; appropriateness of 109;
'emotional literacy' in 124, 125

damage 19, 55, 88, 109, 165
danger 77, 82, 149, 156
Dawson, N. 144
day-dreaming 29
death 89, 90, 116, 152–3, 166; of
father 74, 120–1, 155; of mother
152–3
defences 28, 38, 81, 94, 143, 164;
breaking through 112; latency 12;
threats and 133
delinquency 18, 19
denial 55
dependency 16, 24, 44, 50, 53, 62;
ability to show 74–5; lost 164
depression 19, 42, 96, 163, 166;
clinical, mild 101; measuring the
degree of 100

deprivation 30, 57; emotional 24, 25;
social 24, 25, 26, 31
DES (Department of Education and
Science) 66
desire 8, 166, 170; inhibition and 171;
unconscious 58, 60, 61
despair 82, 93, 159, 163, 164
desperation 72, 113
destructiveness 18, 89, 118
deterioration 39; intellectual 37
development 6, 10, 13, 46, 58, 94, 99,
162; cognitive 43, 75, 124;
emotional 15, 22, 75, 160;
facilitated 19; impeded 23;
infantile 67; maturational 25;
psychological 15, 64; social 64;
staff 157
Dickens, Charles 6–8
differences 76, 138
digestion 143, 144, 149, 155, 156,
157, 162
disabilities 37–51, 66, 135
disapproval 114
disclosures 57, 97
discovery 79, 115
dislocation 154
disruption 13, 16, 91, 97, 119, 126,
145, 157
distance 37–51, 157, 168
distress 46, 47, 72, 92, 94, 108,
153; alleviating 160; assuaging
82; embargo on talking about
157
divorce 40
dogma 128
doubts 15, 16, 18
Dover-Councell, J. 143
drama 87, 88, 89, 92, 93, 94, 171
drawings 27, 76–7, 115, 116, 119–20,
146, 149, 156
dreams 81, 93
drugs 55, 60, 154
Dundas, E. 37
Dyke, S. 143

Earwaker, J. 47
education 14, 17, 59, 112, 120;
individual plans 109, 117–19;
social 116, 124

educational therapy 142, 143, 144,
156
Eliot, T. S. 166
Ellis, Albert 128
emotional difficulties 108, 109, 112,
125, 137, 142; anger a reflection
of 126
'emotional literacy' 124–41
emotionality 15
empathy 38, 39, 160
emptiness 167
enactment 89
encouragement 55, 130
engagement 44–5
environment 9, 71, 79, 83, 127, 163;
control of 84, 89, 91; emotional
82; positive 119; predictable and
secure 85; safe 136; therapeutic
and nurturing 138; see also
facilitating environment; holding
environment
'environmental impingement' 23
envy 9, 18, 72, 126; parental 163
Epictitus 97
'epistemophilic instinct' 8
EPs (educational psychologists)
108–23, 124, 125, 131, 132
'era of industry' 12
Erikson, E. 12
essay-writing 159–74
exclusion 116, 156; risk of 125, 131
expectations 59, 142, 149, 153, 154;
characterised by fear 161–2;
unrealistic 101; unspoken 114
experience 6, 10, 24, 26, 45, 65, 74;
cognitive sorting of 110;
'companion in' 77; concrete 53;
56; emotional 58; in infancy 8, 9,
52; intensive 87; learning from 9;
qualitative 61; 'raw' 67–8;
'scripts' and 114; splitting up of
12; transitional 31; undigested
144; unsorted 'bricks' of 78
exploitation 31, 126
exploration 73, 82, 83, 84, 92, 97, 129
expression 72, 89, 91, 122; symbolic
and physical 121
expressive therapy 37
externalising 144

eye contact 72

facial expressions 133
facilitating environment 23–4, 25, 27,
28, 67
facts 6, 7, 10; hunger for 12
failure 56, 57, 62, 96, 104, 105; anger
at 168; perceived sense of 101
fairy-tales 88, 89, 90
family 17, 23, 40–1, 55, 69, 102;
dependence on 16; learning in
10–11; loosening ties with 15;
marginalisation in 30; nuclear,
intact 101; reflection on 111;
talking about 45
family therapy 144
fantasy 45, 53, 110
fathers 8, 10, 23, 29, 56; death of 74,
120–1, 155; drug addicted 55; love
from 104–5; memories of 45; poor
relationship with daughter 62;
weekends with/visits to 27, 113;
withdrawn and placid 168
fatness 104
Faupel, Adrian 125, 126
fears 18, 28, 41, 42, 72, 77, 78, 169;
about anger 136; bound up with
feelings 126; 'full up' with 81;
inner 90; joining in 148; not
readily assuaged 85; primitive
162; separation 92; unexpressed
74
Figlio, K. 70
Firework Model 127, 132–3
flexibility 43; need for 45–6
formulation 12; assessment and
100–2
'frames' 25
free association 160
freedom 60, 166, 169; unwonted 27
French, Dawn 104
Freud, Sigmund 10, 41, 52, 54, 63,
143
friends 13, 15, 17–18, 43, 47, 48–9,
102; lacking 27, 71
frustration 9, 40, 53, 82, 93, 108, 155,
159; unmet 63

games 129, 132, 135, 146, 154

unconscious life/aspects 54, 67, 69, 88, 89, 110, 163; desire 58, 60, 61; phantasies 162
underachievement 71
understanding 22, 26, 28, 39, 61, 64, 88, 115, 143; anger 127; context aids 144; degrees of 47, 94; empathic 160; false and unhelpful 114; lack of 120; new 67; promoting 112; social interactions 135
unhappiness 29, 62, 81, 101, 102, 109
unpredictability 29, 84
'updating' 83, 84
uselessness 101, 102

values 16
violence 41, 44, 45, 47, 81, 109, 116, 154; domestic or political 142

Waddell, M. 8–9
warm-ups 146–7
Watzlawick, P. 144
weight 104, 155
well-being 87; emotional 97
White, M. 144
Wilson, P. 161
Winnicott, D. W. 22–8 *passim*, 30, 31, 54, 67, 73, 89, 110, 144, 154, 160
wishes 53, 72, 81, 90–1, 111, 148; aggressive 74; and needs 31
withdrawal 76
Woolfe, R. 40
Wooster, G. 163
words 90, 92; not putting feelings into 119
Wordsworth, W. 172
work experience 121
worksheets 132, 133
worries 142, 149, 154, 157